Scottish Place Names

THEIR MEANINGS EXPLAINED

by

Michael Eyers

SPHERE BOOKS LIMITED
30-32 Gray's Inn Road, London WC1X 8JL

Sphere Books Ltd.,
30-32 Gray's Inn Road,
London WC1X 8JL

First published 1980

First published in this edition 1983

© *C.E.S.*

Printed and bound in Great Britain by Collins, Glasgow.

PREFACE

The study of place names is always interesting and those of Scotland have a fascination of their own. The aim of this book is to present, in a simplified form, the true, traditional, probable or possible meanings of as broad a selection of place names as possible, with the hope that this will serve as a useful guide to the visitor to Scotland and to the native Scot alike.

Unfortunately, space does not permit an in-depth analysis of each name; readers who are interested in carrying out their own research will need to study the many books that have already been written on the subject as well as old maps and documents. Anyone who does decide to study the subject seriously will soon find that in addition to being fascinating Scottish place names can be very frustrating because so many of them have undergone change and distortion over the centuries; in many cases the meanings have become uncertain, undecipherable and even *meaningless.* It will also be found that some incorrect meanings have simply been perpetuated through popular tradition because they sound *good* or *romantic.*

As regards the Gaelic speaking areas much distortion has been brought about because of the differences between the spoken and written language; these variations are further complicated by variations in local dialects. This has resulted in many names receiving an anglicised form, giving rise in certain instances to ambiguity and confusion.

In the light of all this it is perhaps not surprising that certain names have aroused a good deal of controversy over the years. Some of this controversy is reflected in this book and readers should therefore not be surprised if sooner or later they come across meanings which differ yet again from those shown here. Variations in spelling should also be expected from time to time.

A.M.E.

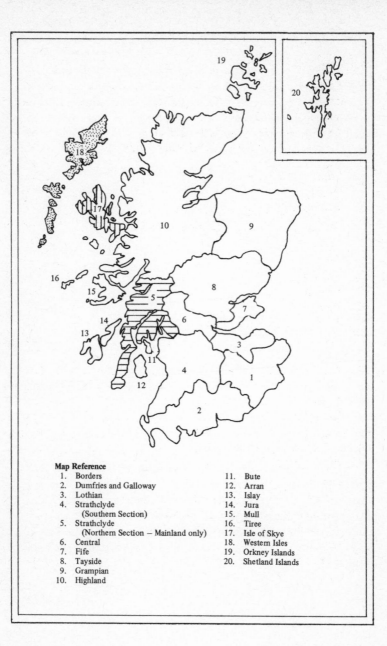

Map Reference

1. Borders
2. Dumfries and Galloway
3. Lothian
4. Strathclyde
   (Southern Section)
5. Strathclyde
   (Northern Section – Mainland only)
6. Central
7. Fife
8. Tayside
9. Grampian
10. Highland
11. Bute
12. Arran
13. Islay
14. Jura
15. Mull
16. Tiree
17. Isle of Skye
18. Western Isles
19. Orkney Islands
20. Shetland Islands

CONTENTS

Readers who wish to study Scottish place names in greater depth will find that there is an abundance of printed material available on the subject, even though some of this may be hidden away in the backs of libraries. Books on place names by the following authors are worth careful reading: W.J.Watson, W.C. Mackenzie, J.B.Johnston and W.F.H.Nicolaisen. Books on Scottish history will yield some interesting background information and it will be found that Blaue's 17th century maps of Scotland provide a useful insight into the older spellings of some names.

LINGUISTIC DISTRIBUTION OF PLACE NAMES

Scotland has been invaded and overrun by different tribes and races during its long history and the migrations of people and languages are reflected in its place names. A detailed analysis is not possible here but the following summary gives a broad outline of the linguistic distribution of place names:

1. In the south-east, especially in the Borders Region, there is a preponderance of English type names.

2. In the south-west, (Dumfries and Galloway, and the southern part of Strathclyde), there is a mixture of Gaelic, Scandinavian and Scots/English names.

3. Names in the Highlands are predominantly Gaelic with a strong Scandinavian influence making itself felt along the western coastline and in the offshore islands.

4. Names in the Western Isles are predominantly Scandinavian.

5. In Orkney, Shetland, and the north-eastern corner of the Highland Region (Caithness) the names are virtually all of Scandinavian origin.

6. To the east of the Central Highlands there are many names of English and Scots origin, together with names which denote territory once occupied by the Picts.

USEFUL BACKGROUND INFORMATION

The Picts. Names beginning with prefixes PIT and PET denote places once inhabited by the Picts, an ancient race about whom historians have limited knowledge. Some of them are believed to have spoken a language which was closely akin to Welsh. Most names in this category are to be found in the Fife, Tayside and Grampian Regions. The suffixes —TY, TIE, DY, DIE tend to be prevalent in what was Pictish territory.

Aber and Inver. Both these names signify *mouth of a river or stream* or the *confluence of two water courses*. Aber, in some instances, has also come to have the meaning of marsh or swamp, e.g. Lochaber — Loch of the Marshes. Readers will immediately recognise Aber as being a prefix that is frequently found in Welsh place names; Inver, however, is distinctly Scottish. Names with Aber are generally to be found in those areas associated with the Picts, namely Fife, Tayside and Grampian. When Aber or Inver denotes the confluence of two water courses it is usually the lesser stream which gives its name to the place, and a careful study will reveal that the place itself is often a little way off from the actual river or stream from which it takes its name.

Old systems of land measure. Many place names indicate the extent of a certain area of land. In the western part of the country an old Scandinavian system of land measure prevailed; the main unit was the ounce-land — the amount of land which paid the rent of an ounce of silver. The ounce-land was generally made up of 20 penny-lands. In some cases these were subdivided into halfpenny-lands, e.g. Lephinmore and Lephinchapel on the side of Loch Fyne, and even into farthing-lands, e.g. Feorline on the Isle of Arran. The Scots penny was generally one twelfth of a penny sterling.

Further east the unit of measure was a davach or davoch which was equated with the ounce-land. The davach was the equivalent of 4 ploughgates (or carucates) and 1 ploughgate was the equivalent of 8 oxgangs (or bovates). A davach was originally a measure of capacity which indicated the yield a farmer obtained from a certain area of land or the quantity of seed he sowed over that area. The area was thus variable but a davach was reckoned to be approximately 104 Scots acres or 120 English acres. In some places we find an interesting subdivision into the half-davach, e.g. the anglicised version of Haddo in the Grampian Region or the Gaelic version of Lettoch (Leth dabhach) in Strathspey. Other subdivisions include a third, e.g. Trinafour near Loch Rannoch, a quarter, and a fifth, e.g. Coigeach near Ullapool. In islay we find a *long eighth* of a davach in Octofad.

The merkland (or mark-land) is also met with in some places and again this seems to have been a variable measure.

Mains of . . . . . or . . . . .**Mains.** This is an abbreviated form of the word *Domains* and is used to denote a farm house on a landed estate as opposed to the house belonging to the laird or landlord.

The ancient British language. Some of the Picts, as already mentioned, are believed to have spoken a language which was closely akin to Welsh. It is known that a Celtic language similar to Welsh (sometimes referred to as British or Cumbrian) was spoken by some of the early inhabitants of Scotland. Traces of this language are still found in certain place names and the following are a few examples:

Lanark corresponds to the Welsh *llanerch* meaning a *glade*.

Lhanbryde (Grampian), Lumphanan (Grampian), Lumphinnans (Fife). The elements *lhan* and *lumph* correspond to the Welsh *llan* meaning an *enclosure* or *church*.

Kincardine (Fife). The second element represents the Welsh *cardden* meaning a *thicket*.

Perth meaning a *bush, grove or copse* is the same word in Welsh.

Pencaitland (Lothian) represents the Welsh *pen + coed + llan*, i.e. *head + wood + enclosure*.

Bathgate (Lothian) is thought by some to mean *boar wood* and to represent the Welsh *baedd + coed*.

Penpont (Dumfries and Galloway) represents two simple Welsh words.

The names Cramond (Lothian), Carstairs (Strathclyde), Cathcart (Glasgow), and Caerlaverock (Dumfries and Galloway) all contain, in one form or another the Welsh word *caer*. Kirkintilloch (Strathclyde) meaning *fort at the head of the hillock* is made up of the Welsh *caer + pen* and the Gaelic *tulach*.

Traquair (Borders) the Ochiltree (Strathclyde) both contain the Welsh *tre(f)* meaning *town or homestead*. In the second name *Ochil* corresponds to the Welsh *uchel* meaning *high*.

Cawdor (Highland) and probably Calder (Lothian) represent the Welsh *caled + dwr* meaning *hard water*.

Trossachs meaning *the cross hills* contains the modern Welsh word *traws*.

Ebb-tide islands. Scattered around the western coastal area are several small islands which bear the names of Orosay, Ornsay and Oronsay. These small islands have one feature in common; they are ebb-tide islands, i.e. islands which have dry access to the mainland or another larger island when the tide is out.

PRONUNCIATION

It is not possible to give a general guide to the pronunciation of Scottish place names as they represent a mixture of different languages, and many have their own special local pronunciation. The rules of Gaelic pronunciation are rather complex but readers will find the following points useful for dealing with those place names which are of Gaelic origin (mostly the Highlands, islands off the west coast and parts of the south west):

BH and MH — usually pronounced as 'V'. However, DUBH (black) is pronounced 'DOO'.

FH — at the beginning of a word is silent, e.g. FHUAR = 'OOAR'.

TH — at the beginning of a word = 'H'.

TH — in the middle or at the end of a word is silent, e.g. STRATH is usually pronounced 'Stra—'; LIATH is pronounced 'LEE—A'.

In place names which contain the element —AN T—S. . the 'S' is silent.

COMMON CELTIC PLACE NAME ELEMENTS
(MOSTLY GAELIC)

Aber (or simply Ar) — the mouth or confluence of a river or
stream.
    Aberdeen — mouth of the River Don.
    Aberlemno — confluence of the elm stream.
    Arbroath — mouth of the River Brothock.

Ach, Auch (a variant of Achadh) — a field.
    Auchintoul — field of the barn.
    Auchnashelloch — field of the willows.
    Achiemore — big field.

Ald, Alt, Auld, Allt, Ault — a burn or stream.
    Aultbea — birch stream, burn of the birch tree.
    Cumbernauld — confluence of the streams.
    Garbhallt — rough stream.

Ard, Aird — a height or headland.
    Ardgour — height of the goats.
    Ardnamurchan — point or headland of the great seas.
    Ardrishaig — height of the briars.

Auchter, Ochter — top, upper part, height.
    Auchterderran — height of the groves, thickets.
    Auchtermuchty — height of the pigs' place.
    Drumochter — ridge of the upper part.

Bad — a clump, grove, thicket.
    Badachro — grove of the sheep fold.
    Badcall — hazel grove.
    Badentarbert — grove of the isthmus.

Bal, Bally, Baile — a homestead, hamlet.
    Balblair — homestead of the plain.
    Balgowan — homestead of the smith.
    Ballencrieff — homestead by the tree.

Bar, Barr — a height, summit.
    Barcaldine — height of the hazel trees.
    Bargrennan — height of the sunny spot.
    Barravullin — height of the mill.

Beg, Beag, Bheag — small, little.
    Beinn bheag — little mountain.
    Ardbeg — little height or headland.
    Carn Beag Dearg — small red cairn.

Blar, Blair — a plain.
    Balblair — homestead of the plain.
    Blairmore — big plain.
    Blairour — dun coloured plain.

Bon, Bun — foot (usually applies to the mouth or confluence of a river or stream).
    Bonawe — mouth of the River Awe.
    Bunnahabhainn —river mouth.
    Bunchrew — foot of the trees.

Breac, Bhreac, Breck, Vrack(ie) — speckled.
    Ben Vrackie — speckled mountain.
    Carn Breac — speckled cairn.
    Creag Bhreac — speckled rock.

Camas, Camus, Cambus — a bay or creek (inland = a bend in the river).
    Cambuslang — boat creek.
    Cambus o' May — bend of the plain.
    Camusdarrach — bay of the oak trees.

Cor, Coire — a corrie, round hollow, circular glen in a mountain side; also a whirlpool.
    Carn a' Choire Mhoir — cairn of the big round hollow.
    Meall a ' Choire Leith — large round hill of the grey round hollow.
    Corrievreckan — whirlpool of Brecan (a legendary figure).

Dal, Dall a field.
   Dalbeattie — field of the birch trees.
   Dalguise — field of the fir trees.
   Dalnaspidal — field of the hospital or hospice.

Dubh, Dou — black or dark.
   Douglas — dark stream.
   Cnoc Dubh — black hillock.
   Barradhu — black height or point.

Dum, Dun — a hill or fort.
   Dumbarton — fort of the Britons.
   Dunmore — big hill.
   Dunlop — hill by the bend.

Eilean — an island.
   Eilean Dubh — black island.
   Eilean Mor — big island.
   Eilean nan Each — island of the horses.

Fionn, Finn — white or clear.
   Findlater — white, clear hillside.
   Findon — white hill.
   Carfin — white rock.

Gleann, Glen — a narrow valley, glen.
   Glenbreck — speckled glen.
   Gleneagles — glen of the church.
   Glendearg — red glen.

Innis, Inch — this word has two meanings: 1. an island;
   2. a meadow by the side of a river.
   Inchkinloch — meadow at the head of the loch.
   Inchnadamph — meadow of the ox.
   Inchtavanach — monk's island.

Inver, Inner — the mouth or confluence of a river or stream.
   Inveraray — mouth of the River Aray.
   Inverness — mouth of the River Ness.
   Innerleithen — confluence of the River Leithen.

Ken, Kin, Ceann – a head. Often used to indicate the top or end of some feature.

   Kinloch – head of the loch.
   Kingussie – end of the pine wood.
   Kenmore – big head or top.

Kil – a church or burial place. Originally a monk's "cell".

   Kilbride – church of St. Bridget.
   Kilninver – church at the river mouth.
   Kilphedir – church of St. Peter.

Knock, Cnoc – a knoll or hillock. Often pronounced "Croc".

   Knockan – little hillock.
   Knockbain – white, fair hillock.
   Knockandu – black little hillock.

Lag – a hollow.

   Laggan – a little hollow.
   Lagavulin – hollow of the mill.

Leth – half.

   Lealt – a half burn or stream, i.e. a burn with sloping land on one side.
   Lephinmore – big halfpenny-land (a reference to an old system of land measure).
   Lettoch – half davach (a reference to an old system of land measure).

Letter – a slope or hillside.

   Letters – hillside.
   Letterfearn –slope of the alder tree.
   Lettermore – big slope.

Loch – this is used to denote either an inland lake or an inlet of the sea. Lochan means *a little loch*.

   Loch Long – loch of ships.
   Loch nan Uamh – loch of the caves.
   Lochan Fada – long little loch.

Mor, Mhor, More — big, large.

    Ben More — big mountain.

    Braemore — large upland.

    Creag Dhubh Mhor — big black rock.

Pit, Pet — a croft or homestead. Generally found in north-eastern Scotland, this prefix is usually associated with places once inhabited by the Picts.

    Pitcaple — homestead of the mare or horse.

    Pitlochry — stony homestead.

    Pittenweem — homestead by the cave.

Pol, Poll — a pit or pool.

    Polgown — pool of the smith.

    Polmont — pool on the hill.

    Poltalloch — pool of the smithy.

Strath — a broad valley. Usually pronounced "Stra—".

    Strathaven — valley of the river.

    Strathmore — large valley.

    Strathkanaird — valley of the River Cainneart.

Sron, Stron — a nose or point.

    Strone.

    Stronachlachar — stonemason's point.

    Strontian — point of the little hill.

Tarbert, Tarbet, Tarbat, Tairbeart, Tairbeirt — an isthmus. This is quite a common name and is usually found associated with places on a narrow strip of land between two lochs.

Tobar, Tobair, Tober, Tiber, Tibber — a well.

    Tobermory — well of Mary.

    Auchentiber — field of the well.

    Knockentibber — hillock of the well.

Tom — a round hillock.

    Tomintoul — hillock of the barn.

    Tomnahurich — hillock of the yew wood.

    Tomnavoulin — hillock of the mill.

COMMON SCANDINAVIAN PLACE NAME ELEMENTS

A, Ay, Ey — an island.
> Bernera — Bjorn's island.
> Eday — isthmus island.
> Sanday — sandy island.

Bolstadr (becomes —Bister, —Busta, —Bost) — a homestead.
> Melbost — homestead by the sandbank.
> Habost — high homestead.
> Grimbister — Grim's homestead.

Breidr — broad.
> Brodick — broad bay.
> Breibister — broad homestead.

Dalr — a dale.
> Langadale — long dale.
> Swordale — grassy dale.

Hop, Hope — a bay.
> Longhope — long bay.
> Oban — little bay (an instance where Gaelic has borrowed a word from the Scandinavian).

Kirkja — a church.
> Kirkwall — church bay.
> Kirkibost — homestead by the church.

Lax — a salmon.
> Laxavat — salmon water.
> Laxdale — salmon dale.

Ness, Nish — a cape, headland or point.
> Aignish — ridge point.
> Arnish — eagle's point.
> Durness — deer cape.

Setr (becomes —sett, —ster, —shader) — a house or dwelling.
> Grimshader — Grim's dwelling.
> Earshader — beach dwelling.

Stadr (becomes —sta) — a farm.
Mealasta — sandbank farm.
Tolsta — Tholf's farm.

Vagr (becomes —wall, —way, —vagh) — a creek or bay.
Carloway — Karl's bay.
Scalloway — bay of the huts or cottages.

Vatn (becomes Vat) — water, lake.
Langavat — long water.
Grunavat — green water.
Breivat — broad water.

Vik, Vig, Vaig — a bay.
Lerwick — mud bay.
Miavaig — narrow bay.

OTHER PLACE NAME ELEMENTS

In the south of Scotland one finds certain reoccurring elements in the names of some hills: RIG — a ridge; KNOWE — a knoll or hillock; CLEUCH — a cleft or ravine; LAW — a hill; FELL — a mountain. A variant of FELL is found in the Western Isles and in the islands off the western coast where some mountain names end in —VAL.

(1.) BORDERS

Abbey St. Bathans —	St. Baothen or Baithene was St. Columba's cousin and his successor as abbot of Iona.
Ancrum —	Bend on the River Ale (Alne).
Ashiesteel —	Place of ash trees.
Auchencrow —	Stream by the trees.
Ayton —	Town on the River Eye.
Berwick (North) —	Barley farm, village.
Blackhaugh —	Black riverside meadow.
Bonjedward —	Confluence of Jed Water (with River Teviot).
Branxholme —	Branoc's home or land.
Broughton —	Town at the fort or hill or town at the brook.
Buccleuch —	Rock homestead, hamlet.
Caldra —	Hard water place, **or** cold place.
Coldingham —	Village of Colud's people or of the people at Colud.
Cowdenburn —	Stream at the back of the hill **or** cow pasture stream.
Darnick —	Hidden dwelling, village.
Duns —	Hills.
Eccles —	A church
Ednam —	Village by Eden Water.
Edrom —	Village by River Adder.
Eyemouth —	Mouth of Eye Water. Eye means "stream".
Galashiels —	Huts on Gala Water.
Glenbreck —	Speckled glen.
Glendearg —	Red glen.
Hawick —	High dwelling **or** enclosed dwelling, village.
Innerleithen —	Confluence of Leithen Water (with River Tweed).
Jedburgh —	Fenced in homestead on the River Jed.
Kelso —	Chalk height, ridge.

Lammermuir –	Lambs moor.
Lauder –	Town on the foaming river or canal.
Leitholm –	Village on Leet Water.
Linton –	Pool or stream town.
Marchmont –	Named after the 1st Earl of Marchmont (literally "Border hill").
Maxton –	Maccus' town.
Melrose –	Bare moor.
Midlem –	Middle homestead, village.
Morebattle –	Lakeside dwelling.
Oxnam –	Village of the oxen.
Peebles –	Tents, pavilions.
Roxburgh –	Hroc's fort, town or possibly "Rook's town".
Ruthven –	Red rock.
Saughtree –	Probably simply "A willow tree".
St. Abbs –	Named after St. Ebba, a daughter of King Ethelfrith.
St. Boswells –	St. Boswell or Boisil was Prior at a local monastery founded in the 7th century.
Selkirk –	Church of the hall or dwelling.
Smailholm –	Small or narrow village **or** village of the small cattle.
Thirlestane –	Stone with a hole.
Threepwood –	Disputed wood.
Traquair –	Village on Quair Water.
Tweedsmuir –	Moor by the River Tweed.
Yarrow –	Rough water.
Yetholm –	Village at the gate or pass (between England and Scotland).

Applegarth — Apple orchard.
Auchencairn — Field of the cairn.
Auchenleck — Field of the flat stones.
Auchentibbert — Field of the well.
Auldgirth — Old garden.

Balmaclellan — Maclellan's town or manor (attributed to John Maclellan who obtained a charter from King James III in 1466).
Bargrennan — Sunny height.
Borgue — A fort or stronghold.
Brydekirk — Church of St. Bridget.
Buittle — House or dwelling place.
Caerlaverock — Fortress of Llywarch Og.
Cairn Edward Forest — So called because Edward, brother of Robert the Bruce, built a cairn on a hill here.
Capplegill — Glen or ravine of the chapel.
Carsphairn — Low lying land of the alder trees by the river.
Castle Douglas — Named in 1792 after Sir William Douglas of Gelston Castle.
Challock — The forge or furnace.
Clachaneasy — Village by the waterfall **or** village of the church of Jesus.
Corrie — A circular glen.
Corriedoo — Dark circular glen.
Craigcleuch — Rock of the ravine or cleft.
Craigdarroch — Rock of the oak wood.
Crawick — Probably, crow's dwelling or place.
Creca — A rock.
Creetown — Town on the River Cree (Cree = a boundary, i.e. between East and West Galloway).
Crossmichael — Cross of St. Michael **or** big cross.
Cummertrees — Possibly, confluence among the thorns.
Dalbeattie – Field of the birch trees.

Dalfibble —	Field of the tents, pavilions.
Dalgarnock —	Field of the noisy little stream.
Dalry —	King's field.
Dalton —	Fort or town in the dale.
Drumbuie —	Yellow ridge.
Drummore —	Big ridge.
Drumwalt —	Grassy ridge.
Dumfries —	Hill or fort of the thicket.
Duncow —	Hill or fort of the hazel.
Dunscore —	Hill or fort with the rampart.
Durisdeer —	Probably, thorn land.
Ecclefechan —	Little church **or** St. Fechin's church (St. Fechin or Vigeanus founded various churches in Ireland).
Galloway —	Land of the stranger-Gael.
Garlieston —	Town founded by Lord Garlies, the 7th Earl of Galloway.
Garraries —	Small summer residences.
Gillenbie —	Ravine town.
Girthon —	Garden or enclosure on the river (Fleet).
Glengaber —	Glen of the goats.
Glenluce —	Glen of the water of herbs or plants.
Glentrool —	Probably, glen of the stream.
Gretna —	Probably, a gravel hollow.
Heck —	A gate.
Haugh of Urr —	Flat meadow by Urr Water.
Kildrochat —	Church by the bridge.
Kirkbean —	Probably, the church of St. Bean.
Kirkchrist —	Christchurch.
Kirkcolm —	Church of St. Colm/Columba.
Kirkconnel —	Church of St. Conval/Conal.
Kirkcowan —	Church of St. Comhgan.
Kirkcudbright —	Church of St. Cuthbert (Bishop of Lindisfarne).
Kirkgunzeon —	Church of St. Wynnin.
Kirkinner —	Church of St. Kennera.

Kirkpatrick Durham —	Church of St. Patrick (with the addition of the family name of Durham — probably an early proprietor).
Kirkpatrick Fleming —	Church of St. Patrick (with the addition of the family name Fleming — traditionally that of a former landowner who came over from Belgium in the 14th century).
Kirkpatrick Irongray —	Church of St. Patrick of the cattle land.
Kirkpatrick Juxta —	Church of St. Patrick adjacent (to Moffat).
Lag —	A hollow.
Lagganmullan —	Little hollow of the mill.
Lang holm —	Long village or water meadow.
Laurieston —	Lawrence's town. Said to be derived from the name of an 18th century landowner.
Laverhay —	Leofhere's enclosure.
Leswalt —	Grass enclosure.
Lochinch —	Loch of the island or water meadow.
Lochmaben —	Loch in the white plain **or** Loch or stone of Mabon (a British prince) **or** Loch or stone of Maponus (a Celtic deity).
Lockerbie —	Probably, Lockhart's Town. The Lockharts held land here in the 14th century.
Luce (New) —	Named after the river on which it stands. (Luce means plant or herb).
Mennock —	A monk. (a monastery is said to have existed here at one time).
Merkland —	A mark-land (reference to old system of land measure).
Middlebie —	Middle town.
New Abbey —	So called to distinguish it from the old abbey at Dundrennan.

Newton Stewart —	New town of William Stewart, 3rd son of the Earl of Galloway.
Penpont —	Hill of the bridge.
Polgown —	Pool or bog of the smith.
Port William —	Founded by Sir William Maxwell in 1770.
Portyerrock —	Harbour by the rocks.
Sanquhar —	Old fort or town.
Sibbaldbie —	Sibbald's homestead or village.
Spittal —	A hospital or hospice.
Stewartry —	An alternative name for Kirkcudbright-shire. So called because because the area was once under the jurisdiction of a royal steward.
Stoneykirk —	Stony field.
Stroan —	A streamlet.
Threave —	A house or village.
Tinwald —	Assembly field.
Torthorwald —	Torthar's wood or Thorald's hill.
Tynron —	House on the point.
Wamphray —	Probably a den or hollow in the forest.
Whithorn —	White house.
The Wig —	The bay.
Wigtown —	Town on the bay **or** Wicga's farm **or** a homestead.

(3.) LOTHIAN

Abercorn —	Horned confluence.
Aberlady —	Marsh or river mouth or the rotton smell (a reference to rotting fish in former times)
Armadale —	Named after Lord Armadale.
Athelstaneford —	Said to be connected with the Saxon king Athelstan who fought a battle against the Picts in the 10th century.
Balerno —	Barley farm.
Ballencrieff —	Homestead by the tree.
Bathgate —	Boar wood **or** cottage by the wood.
Blackburn —	Black stream.
Blackness —	Black headland.
Bolton —	Enclosed dwelling.
Broxburn —	Probably badger's stream.
Calder (E., W., Mid) —	Hard water (reference to a stream) **or** a cool place.
Cockburnspath —	Colbrand's path (from an old personal name).
Cramond —	Fort on the River Almond.
Currie —	A fen **or** bog.
Dalkeith —	Meadow of the wood.
Dunbar —	Hill fort.
Dundas —	South hill.
Ecclesmachan —	Church of St. Machan.
Edinburgh —	The fortress of Eidyn.
Fauldhouse —	House on unploughed land.
Garvald —	Rough stream.
Gilston —	Gille's farm, dwelling.
Haddington —	Dwelling place of Hadda's people.
Hedderwick —	Heather dwelling.
Joppa —	Named after Joppa in Palestine.
Kirkliston —	Church of Lissa's town.
Liberton —	Possibly, lepers' town, but this is disputed.
Linlithgow —	Possibly, a lake in a damp hollow.
Livingston —	Leving's dwelling.
Loanhead —	Top of the lane.

Longniddry —	Possibly, the church or enclosure by the new house.
Morham —	Village on the moor.
Muirhouses —	Moor houses.
Musselburgh —	Mussel town. There are mussel beds just off-shore.
Newbattle —	New building. This is a reference to the abbey founded in 1140 and said to have been named thus to distinguish it from the *old building*.
Ochiltree —	High dwelling place.
Oldhamstocks —	Old dwelling place.
Ormiston —	Orme's **or** Ormr's dwelling.
Pencaitland —	Head **or** hill of the wooded enclosure.
Pitcox —	Homestead of the fifth part.
Portobello —	Said to be so named after a town in Panama. A Scottish sailor who claimed to have been present at Admiral Vernon's victory there in 1739 gave this name to his house around which the resort grew.
Prestonpans —	Priest's village of the salt pans. (Salt-panning was carried out here by the monks of Newbattle Abbey in the 12th century).
Ratho —	Mounds **or** forts.
South Queensferry —	Named after Queen Margaret, wife of Michael Canmore, who often passed through here.
Straiton —	Town on the Roman road.
Temple —	This was formerly the seat of the Knights Templar in Scotland.
Tyninghame —	The village of the people on the Tyne.
Whitburn —	White stream.

(4.) STRATHCLYDE
(SOUTHERN SECTION)

Alloway —	Probably, a rocky place.
Arbuckle —	Height of the shepherd.
Ardeer —	West cape.
Ardrossan —	Height of the little headland **or** height of the horses (possibly a reference to Horse Isle off-shore).
Auchenbothie —	Field of the cottage.
Auchengray —	Field of the herd.
Auchentiber —	Field of the well.
Auchinleck —	Field of the flat stones.
Ayr —	Meaning uncertain. Possibly, a gravelly beach.
Balgray —	Homestead of the herd.
Ballantrae —	Homestead **or** village on the shore.
Balloch —	A pass.
Barlinnie —	Height of the pool.
Barr —	A height **or** hill.
Bearsden —	Named after a house near the railway station which was opened in 1863.
Beith —	A beech tree.
Biggar —	Probably, a barley field.
Blair —	A plain.
Blairquhanan —	Plain of the canon **or** dog.
Cambuslang —	Boat creek.
Cambusnethan —	Creek of Nethan **or** Nechtan.
Carfin —	White stone.
Carmunnock —	A hill fort **or** monks' fort.
Carluke —	Probably, the church of St. Moluag or St. Lesc. (A name which has undergone considerable change).
Carmyle —	A bare, round rock.
Carnwath —	Cairn **or** mound in the wood.
Carrick —	A rock.
Carstairs —	Castle of Tarres.
Cathcart —	Castle on the Cart River.

Cleghorn —	Clay house **or** house by the haystack.
Clock Point —	Stone point.
Coatbridge —	Bridge by the cottages.
Coulter —	The lying-back land.
Covington —	Colban's town.
Cowcaddens —	Wood **or** nook of hazels.
Craigdarroch —	Rock of the oak trees.
Crawfordjohn —	Crow's ford. Founded by John, a stepson of Baldwin.
Cumbernauld —	A confluence of streams.
Cumnock —	Valley of the hillock.
Dalbair —	Field of the plain.
Dalmuir —	Big field.
Dalry —	Field of the king.
Dolphinton —	Dalfine's town. Dalfine was a brother of the 1st Earl of Dunbar.
Douglas —	Dark stream.
Dreghorn —	Probably, a dry house.
Dunlop —	Hill at the bend.
Duntocher —	Hill **or** fort by the causeway.
Eaglesham —	Meaning uncertain. Possibly, a church hamlet **or** a church in the low lying meadow.
Fenwick —	Marsh dwelling **or** village.
Gartcosh —	Cave enclosure.
Girvan —	Possibly, place of rough water.
Glasgow —	A green hollow **or** a dear green place.
Glespin —	Probably, green penny — land.
Gourock —	A rough **or** round hillock.
Greenock —	A sunny place **or** hillock, **or** a green bay.
Hamilton —	Formerly called Cadzow. Renamed in 1445 by the first Lord Hamilton.
Houston —	Hugh's town. Named after Hugo de Pavinan who held lands here in the 12th century.
Inchinnan —	St. Finnan's meadow.
Kilbarchan —	Church of St. Barchan **or** Berchan.
Kilbride (East/West) —	Church of St. Bridget.

27

Kilmacolm –	Church of St. Malcolm **or** of my Colm, Columba.
Kilmarnock –	Church of St. Marnoc.
Kilmaurs –	Church of St. Maurus **or** Maura.
Kilsyth –	Church of St. Syth.
Kilwinning –	Church of St. Wynnin (a variant of Finnan).
Kirkintilloch –	Fort at the head of the hillock.
Kirkoswald –	Church of St. Oswald.
Knockentiber –	Hillock of the well.
Kyle –	A narrow passage **or** strait.
Lanark –	A glade.
Largs –	Slopes.
Lesmahagow –	Church of St. Mahago **or** Machuti.
Lochwinnoch –	Loch full of birds, **or** Loch of St. Winnoc **or** Wynnin (Finnan).
Mauchline –	Plain with a pool.
Maybole –	Maiden's dwelling.
Milngavie –	A windmill, **or** a windy hill.
Moscow –	Hazel field.
Muirkirk –	Moor church.
Newbigging –	New building.
Newton Mearns –	New town in the Stewartry, i.e. an area administered by a steward.
Ochiltree –	High town **or** village.
Paisley –	Probably, a church. Thought to be a corrupted variant of Basilica.
Patna –	Named after a city in India.
Pettinain –	Possibly, a homestead by the river **or** a clear open space.
Pinmore –	Big penny-land.
Pinwherry –	Probably, penny-land of the copse.
Prestwick –	Priest's dwelling.
Renfrew –	Headland of the stream.
Riccarton –	Richard's town.
Saltcoats –	Salt workers' cottages.
Shettleston –	Villa of Sadin's son.

Shotts –	Steep slopes.
Sorn –	A kiln.
Stair –	Stepping stones (over a bog or river)
Straiton –	Town on the Roman road **or**
	hill pasture town.
Strathaven –	Valley of the river.
Symington –	Simon's town.
Torrance –	Probably, a little hill or mound.
Troon –	A headland.
Wishaw –	Probably, a willow wood.

Achnahoish –	Field of the cave **or** hollow.
Achadhchaorunn –	Field of the mountain ash.
Achahoish –	Field of the deer, stag.
Achaleven –	Field of the elm trees.
Achnacroish –	Field of the cross.
Achnamara –	Field of the sea.
Alexandria –	Named about 1760 after Alexander Smollett, M.P., of Bonhill.
Appin –	Abbey lands.
Ardchattan –	Height of Abbot Cattan, a friend of St. Columba.
Arddarroch –	Height of the oak trees.
Ardentinny –	Height of the fire.
Ardfern –	Height of the alder trees.
Ardincaple –	Height of the mare.
Ardlamont –	Height of Lamont – a local clan name meaning *lawman*.
Ardrishaig –	Height of the briars.
Arrochar –	A carucate (reference to an old system of land measure).
Auchenlochan –	Field of the little loch.
Ballimeanoch –	Middle homestead.
Balloch –	A pass.
Ballochroy –	Probably, the red pass **or** gap.
Balnagowan (Eilean) –	Island of the smith's homestead.
Barcaldine –	Height of the hazel trees.
Barravullin –	Hill **or** height of the mill.
Benderloch –	Mountain between two lochs.
Blairmore –	Big field **or** plain.
Bonawe –	Foot (or mouth) of the River Awe.
Bonhill –	Meaning uncertain. Probably, house by the stream.
Braevallich –	Upland of the stream.
Cairndow –	Black stone.
Campbeltown –	Named after Archibald Campbell, 7th Earl of Argyll.

Cardross —	Thicket by the headland.
Carradale —	Copse dale.
Carrick —	A rock **or** cliff.
Clachan —	A hamlet with a church.
Clachbreck —	Speckled stone.
Claonaig —	Meandering creek **or** bay.
Claonairigh —	Inclining hill, pasture **or** summer residence.
Colintraive —	The swimming channel **or** narrows. So called because in former days cattle from Bute were made to swim across to the mainland.
Corranbuie —	Yellow low cape.
Craigendoran —	Rock of the otter.
Dalavich —	Field of the River Avich.
Dalness —	Meadow of the waterfall.
Dippen —	Twopenny-land.
Drisheag —	Place of briars.
Druimdrishaig —	Ridge of briars.
Drumlembie —	Ridge of the elm of trees, **or** lamb hill ridge.
Dumbarton —	Fort **or** hill of the Britons.
Dunmore —	Big hill **or** fort.
Dunollie Castle —	Fort of Onlach, Ollach **or** Olaf.
Dunoon —	Fort **or** hill by the river **or** fort of the ash trees.
Dunstaffnage —	Fort of the headland of the staff.
Duror —	Hard or rocky water.
Edentaggart —	Hill brow of the priest.
Fasnacloich —	Dwelling by the rock.
Furnace —	There was once a smelting works here.
Gallanach —	Place full of boughs, branches **or** place full of pillars, standing stones.
Garbhallt —	Rough stream.
Garelochhead —	Head of the short loch.
Gartocharn —	Field of the cairn.
Glasdrum —	Green **or** grey ridge.
Glenbranter —	Possibly, glen of the poor land **or** glen of the black water.

Helensburgh —	Named after Lady Helen, wife of Sir James Colquhoun of Luss.
Hunter's Quay —	Named after a Mr. Hunter who built a pier here.
Inchmurrin —	Traditionally, the island of St. Mirrin.
Inchtavanach —	Monk's Island.
Inveraray —	Mouth of the river of worship, adoration.
Inverchaolain —	Probably, mouth of the narrow river.
Inveroran —	Mouth of the otter stream.
Inveruglas —	Mouth of the dark stream.
Kames	A bay or creek.
Keil/Kiel —	A church.
Kilbrandon —	Church of St. Brandon or Brendan (a friend of St. Columba).
Kilbride —	Church of St. Bridget.
Kilchenzie —	Church of St. Cainnech or St. Kenneth, an associate of St. Columba.
Kilchoan —	Church of St. Comgan or Comhgan.
Kilchrennan —	Meaning uncertain. Possibly, church of St. Adamnan.
Kilchrist —	Church of Christ.
Kilchurn —	Strait at the cairn.
Kilcreggan —	Church on the little rock.
Killeonan —	Church of St. Adamnan.
Kilmartin —	Church of St. Martin (of Tours).
Kilmelford —	Church of the sand bank bay.
Kilmahumaig —	Church of St. Cummoc or Cumine. He was one of the predecessors of St. Adamnan in the abbacy of Iona.
Kilmichael —	Church of St. Michael.
Kilmun —	Church of St. Mun, Mund or Fintan Munnu.
Kilninver —	Church at the river mouth.
Kintyre —	Head of land.
Knapdale —	Dale of the little hill.
Largiemore —	Place of the large slopes.
Lennoxtown —	Town of the elm tree forest.
Lephinchapel —	Halfpenny — land of the horse.
Lephinmore —	Big halfpenny-land.

Lismore –	Great garden **or** fort.
Lochgilphead –	Head of the chisel loch.
Lorn –	Named after the first kind of the Scots in Dalriada.
Luss –	Generally believed to mean *plant* **or** *herb* and so named either from the river of the same name, or, if local legend is correct, on account of the sweet smelling herb which grew on St. Kessog's grave.
Macharioch –	Brindled **or** drab sandy plain.
Machrahanish –	Sandy plain by the headland.
Melfort –	Sandbank bay.
Muasdale –	Mouse **or** moss dale.
Oban –	The little bay.
Ormsary –	Orm's summer residence.
Otter Ferry –	Ferry by the sandbank.
Peninver –	Penny-land by the river mouth.
Pennyfuir –	Penny-land of the pasture.
Poltalloch –	Stream by the forge.
Port Driseach –	Port by the place of the briars.
Portinnisherrich –	Port of the foal's island.
Portnacroish –	Port of the cross.
Renton –	Named by the local M.P., Alexander Smollett of Bonhill, in honour of his wife, Cecilia Renton.
Rhu –	A point **or** cape.
Rosneath –	Headland of the church land **or** sanctuary **or** bare headland.
Saddell –	Sand dale.
Skipness –	Ship headland.
Slockavullin –	Hollow **or** ditch of the mill.
Soroba –	Mud **or** swamp town.
Strachur –	Valley of the meandering river.
Strone –	A point.
Taychreggan –	House by the rocks.
Tayinloan –	House by the marsh **or** meadow.
Taynuilt –	House by the stream.
Tayvallich –	House at the pass **or** gap.
Tighnabruaich –	House on the upland.

Tullich —	The hillock.
Tullochgorm —	Green hillock.
Tynribbie —	House of ensnaring.

(6.) CENTRAL

Aberfoyle —	Confluence of the deep water.
Alloa —	Rocky place.
Auchenbowie —	Field of the cottage, hut.
Auchrioch —	Grey, brindled field.
Balfron —	Homestead in the sheltered hill country.
Balmaha —	Homestead of St. Maha **or** Tatha (one of St. Patrick's companions).
Bannockburn —	White stream.
Bo'ness —	Headland of the fortified town (a corruption of Borrowstounness).
Braeval —	Upland of the homestead.
Breadalbane —	Upper part of Alban.
Brig O'Turk —	Bridge of the wild boar.
Buchanan —	Canon's seat **or** house.
Cambusbarron —	Bend **or** channel of the baron.
Cauldhame —	Cold home (i.e. an empty house set aside for use by travellers in days gone by).
Clackmannan —	Stone of Manau **or** Mannan (a legendary figure).
Drymen —	A ridge **or** hill.
Dunblane —	Hill of Blathainn **or** Blann.
Dunmore —	Big hill **or** fort.
Falkirk —	Speckled church.
Gartmore —	Large field, enclosure.
Gartness —	Field **or** enclosure by the waterfall.
Glenfalloch —	Glen of concealment, hiding.
Inverarnan —	Confluence of Arnain Burn and River Falloch.
Inversnaid —	Mouth of the Needle (stream).
Killin —	White church.
Kinbuck —	Buck's head.
Kinlochard —	Head of the high loch.
Kippen —	Place of decayed tree stumps.
Laggan —	A little hollow.
Larbert —	Probably a *half-copse*.
Laurieston —	Lawrence's town (named after Sir Lawrence Dundas).

Polmont —	Stream, pool **or** bog on the high moor.
Rowardennan —	Point of the height of St. Adamnan (9th Abbot of Iona and biographer of St. Columba).
Slamannan —	Mountain, moor of Manau **or** Mannan (a legendary figure).
Stenhousemuir —	Moor of the stone house.
Stirling —	Enclosure **or** land by the stream.
Strathblane —	Valley of the little flowers.
Strathyre —	Valley of the land **or** western valley.
Stronachlachar —	Stonemason's point.
Tillycoultry —	Hillock on the back of the land.
Trossachs —	The cross hills.
Tullich —	The hillock.
Tyndrum —	House of the ridge.

(7.) FIFE

Auchterderran —	Height of the groves, thickets.
Auchtermuchty —	Height of the pigs' place.
Auchtertool —	Top of the knoll, hillock.
Aberdour —	Mouth of the water.
Baldinnie —	Homestead near the height.
Balgonie —	Homestead of the smith.
Ballingry —	Homestead of the garden **or** wall.
Cardenden —	Hollow by the thicket.
Colinsburgh —	Named after Colin Lindsay, 3rd Earl of Balcarres.
Cowdenbeath —	Possibly means at the back of the birch hill.
Crail —	Fort on the steep rock.
Cults —	Woods.
Dairsie —	An elevated place **or** a place of oak trees **or** a place of brightness.
Dunfermline —	Possibly, hill of the winding stream.
Dysart —	A deserted place, i.e. solitary retreat for a monk.
Falkland —	Falconry land.
Fife —	Traditionally named after FIB, son of Cruithne.
Freuchie —	Heathery place.
Halbeath —	Birchwood.
Kelty —	Hard water.
Kilconquhar —	Probably the church of St. Conchobar **or** Conchar.
Kilrenny —	Church of St. Irenaeus (former Bishop of Lyons).
Kincardine —	Head of the thicket.
Kinglassie —	Head of the stream.
Kingskettle —	King's battlefield, i.e., battlefield to which the name *Kings,* referring to a gift of the lands by King Malcolm IV, was later added.
Kinloch —	Head of the loch.
Kirkcaldy —	City of the strong fort **or** fortress by the well sheltered harbour.
Leuchars —	Place of rushes.

Leven —	Elm water.
Lochgelly —	Bright, clear loch.
Lumphinnans —	Church of St. Finnan (a disciple of St. Mungo).
Pittenweem —	Homestead by the cave.
Strathmiglo —	Valley of the swine **or** valley of the bog loch.
Wemyss —	Caves.

Aberargie —	Confluence of the River Farg (with the Earn).
Aberdaigie —	Confluence of the stream among the thorns.
Aberfeldy —	Confluence of the water-sprite.
Aberlemno —	Confluence of the elm stream.
Abernethy —	Confluence of the River Nethy (with the Earn).
Aberuthven —	Confluence of Ruthven Water (with the Earn).
Aldclune —	Stream of the green pasture.
Amulree —	Maelrubha's ford (i.e. St. Maelrubha).
Angus —	A district name taken from the tribal name Oengus, which in turn is based on an old personal name.
Arbirlot —	Confluence of Elliott Water (with Rottenraw Burn).
Arbroath —	Mouth of the River Brothock.
Ardeonaig —	Height of Adamnan (i.e. St. Adamnan).
Arngask —	Height of the crossing.
Auchterarder —	Upland of the high stream.
Balfour —	Homestead of the pasture.
Balgray —	Homestead of the herd.
Ballindean —	Homestead of the hillock **or** fortress.
Ballinluig —	Homestead of the hollow **or** dell.
Ballintuim —	Homestead of the hillock.
Balnaguard —	Homestead of the tinkers, craftsmen.
Blair Atholl —	Plain of Atholl.
Blairgowrie —	Plain of the goat.
Brechin —	Named after Brychan, **or** Brecan, a legendary Celtic figure.
Broughty Ferry —	Ferry at the place of the bank **or** rampart.
Burghill —	Road by the chapel.
Careston —	Traditionally believed to mean *The Stone of Carald,* which commemorates a Danish leader of that name slain in 1012.
Charleston —	Named after Charles Henderson, a local landowner.

Clova –	Probably the mound at the ford.
Cortachy –	Probably an enclosure.
Crieff –	A tree.
Dalguise –	Field of the fir trees.
Dalnaspidal –	Field of the hospital **or** hospice.
Douglastown –	Named in 1790 after William Douglas, a local man associated with the development of spinning.
Dowally –	Black meadow.
Dull –	A field **or** fort on the Tay.
Dundee –	South hill fort (a reference to Dundee Law) **or** hill of God.
Dunkeld	Fort of the Caledonians **or** hill of the hazels.
Dunnichen –	Hill of Nechtan (King of the Picts).
Edradynate –	Between the refuges **or** between two ravines.
Fowlis –	Place of the lesser stream.
Friochheim –	Freok's **or** Freke's home. Freok is an old personal name to which the German word *heim* was added in 1820.
Gellyburn –	White **or** shining stream.
Gleneagles –	Glen of the church.
Grandtully –	Thicket on the hill.
Inchbare –	Meadow of the wild animal **or** meadow of the well **or** water.
Inverarity –	Confluence of Cobbie Burn and Arity Water. Arity possibly means *slow*.
Inverkeilor –	Confluence of the hard water.
Kenmore –	Big head.
Killiecrankie –	Wood of the aspens.
Kinloch –	Head of the loch.
Kinloch Rannoch –	Head of the fern loch.
Kinnaird –	High point.
Kinross –	Head of the promontory.
Kirriemuir –	Big quarter, i.e., a reference to one of the old territorial divisions of Angus.

Leitfie —	A broad **or** flat place.
Lundie —	Dark water **or** pool.
Meigle —	Bog meadow.
Methven —	Middle stone.
Milnacraig —	The mill of the barony of Craig.
Moness —	Foot of the waterfall.
Montrose —	Moss **or** moor on the headland.
Murroes —	Moor-houses.
Muthill —	A soft place.
Panbride —	The house **or** hollow of St. Bridget.
Pennan —	Little head **or** headland.
Perth —	A copse.
Pitcairn —	Homestead with a cairn.
Pitlochry —	Stony homestead.
Presnerb —	Roe copse.
Rattray —	Fort dwelling **or** village.
Rescobie —	Point of the place of thorns **or** prickles.
Ruthven —	Probably, red rock **or** red river.
Shanzie —	House by the narrow spit of land.
Strathmore —	Big valley.
Tibbermore —	Big well **or** well of Mary.
Tighnablair —	House of the plain.
Tomphubill —	Hillock of the tent, pavilion.
Tressait —	Battle place.
Trinafour —	Pasture land of a third of a davach (reference to an old system of land measure).
Weem —	A cave **or** hollow.

(9.) GRAMPIAN

Aberchirder —	Confluence of the dark stream.
Aberdeen —	Mouth of the River Don.
Aberdour (New) —	Confluence of the water.
Aboyne —	River of the white cow.
Auchallater —	Field of the hard water.
Achnahannet —	Field of the mother church.
Alford —	Probably, high ford.
Auchidoir —	Field of the grove **or** field of the pursuit.
Auchleven —	Field of the elm tree.
Balmoral —	Homestead of the bailiff **or** homestead of the big clearing.
Balnaboth —	Village of the huts.
Banchory —	A monastery.
Banchory Devenick —	The monastery of St. Devenick.
Banff —	Possibly, from an old river name - pig river, **or** from the area - place of hills **or** mountains.
Belhelvie —	Fortunate **or** prosperous homestead.
Bin Forest —	Forest of the hills.
Birse —	A bush **or** thicket.
Blairmore —	Big field **or** plain.
Braemar —	Height of Mar, i.e., the ancient province of Mar. The full name is Castleton of Braemar.
Brideswell —	Probably, well of St. Bridget.
Brodie —	A ditch **or** dyke.
Buchan —	Said to be derived from the Celtic word for a cow.
Buckie —	A small hillock **or** named after the Buck river.
Cabrach —	A copse **or** thicket.
Cairnie —	A thicket **or** a rocky place.
Cambus O'May —	Crook of the plain.
Charlestown of Aberlour —	Town of the loud river confluence (laid out by Charles Grant in 1812).

Clashindarroch (Forest) —	Furrow **or** ditch of the oak trees.
Clatt —	A hidden **or** sheltered place **or** a rocky place.
Cluny —	A green pasture.
Cobairdy —	Hill-back with an enclosed pasture.
Corse —	A cross.
Cottown —	Cottage town, i.e., where cottars **or** farm workers lived.
Coull —	A corner **or** nook.
Coynachie —	Place of assembly **or** meeting.
Craigellachie —	Rock of accusation **or** the echoing rock.
Craigendarroch —	Rock of the oak trees.
Craigievar —	The uppermost rock.
Craiglich —	Rock of the flat stone.
Crathie —	A bare rock.
Crimond —	Boundary hill.
Cromar —	Sheep fold of Mar, i.e., the ancient province of Mar.
Cullen —	(River mouth of) the little nook **or** of the holly.
Cults —	Woods.
Cuminestown —	Founded in 1763 by Joseph Cumine.
Dallas —	Field of the resting place **or** dwelling.
Dandaleith —	Hill with two slopes.
Deer (Old/New) —	Probably, a grove **or** thicket. Before 1722 the name was Auchreddie — the field of the bog myrtle.
Drumbain —	White **or** fair ridge.
Drumblade —	Ridge of flowers.
Drumin —	A ridge **or** hill.
Dufftown —	Founded in 1817 by James Duff, 4th Earl of Fife.
Duffus —	Dark water.
Dumeath —	Possibly, a fertile field.
Durno —	A stony place.
Durris —	Water place.
Dyce —	Southwards.

Dyke —	A ditch, drain **or** dyke.
Echt —	Possibly, an elevated place.
Edintore —	A hill face.
Elgin —	Meaning obscure. Possibly, a hunting place **or** noble place.
Ellon —	An island **or** meadow.
Elrick —	Place of ambush, i.e., a defile for trapping and killing deer.
Fettercairn —	Field **or** slope of the thicket.
Fetteresso Forest —	Field **or** slope of the waterfall.
Findlater —	White **or** clear hillside.
Findhorn —	White **or** clear Earn (the river on which the town stands).
Findon —	White **or** clear hill. Gives the name to Finnan haddocks.
Fochabers —	A pond **or** meadow by the marsh.
Fordoun —	A hill **or** fort by the field or forest.
Forres —	Probably, water's edge (origin uncertain).
Foveran —	A well **or** fountain, supposedly a reference to a spring which once supplied Foveran Castle.
Fraserburgh —	Fraser's town. Named after Sir Alexander Fraser of Philorth in 1601.
Garioch —	Rough ground.
Garmouth —	Probably, a short stretch of flat land.
Gartly —	Enclosure of the hillock.
Glenlivet —	Probably, flood river.
Grange —	A farm.
Haddo —	Half davach. (Reference to an old system of land measure).
Huntly —	Named after an Earl of Huntly who took his name from a place called Huntlie in Berwickshire.
Inverallochy —	Beautiful river mouth **or** river mouth at the rocky place.
Inverlochy —	Dark confluence.
Inverurie —	Confluence of the River Urie (with the River Don).

Kildrummy —	Head **or** end of the ridge.
Kincardine o'Neil —	Head of the thicket of O'Neil.
King Edward —	Head of the division.
Kinloss —	Head of the loch.
Kintore —	Head of the mound **or** head of the manure field.
Kirkhill of Kennethmont —	According to tradition, King Kenneth is buried in the old churchyard located on a mount.
Kirkton of Culsalmond —	Church town at the end of the hill lands.
Kirkton of Logie Buchan —	Church town of the hollow of Buchan (family/territorial name).
Kirkton of Maryculter —	Church town of the back land dedicated to St. Mary. (Reference to a chapel built by the Templars in honour of St. Mary, patron of their order).
Kirkton of Auchterless —	Church town of the upland enclosure **or** garden.
Knock —	A hillock.
Knockando —	A dark **or** black hillock **or** market hill.
Knockandu —	A dark **or** black hillock.
Laggan —	A little hollow.
Lhanbryde —	Church of St. Bridget.
Lochindorb —	Possibly, fishing loch.
Lonmay —	Marsh **or** meadow of the plain.
Lossiemouth —	Possibly, mouth of the herb river.
Lumphanan —	Church of St. Finnan (a disciple of St. Mungo).
Lyne of Skene —	Meadow **or** enclosure of Skene (family name).
Lynturk —	Pool of the wild boar.
Macduff —	Formerly called Doune. Renamed by James Duff, 2nd Earl of Fife in the 18th century.
Maud —	Probably, a soft **or** damp place.
Meldrum —	Ridge of the hill.
Methlick —	Probably, soft, marshy ground by a river.

Midmar —	Bog of Mar (old territorial name).
Migvie —	A boggy place.
Moray —	Probably, a place by the seaside.
Mortlach —	A big hillock.
Moss of Barmuckity —	Moss of the pig's height.
New Machar —	Named after St. Machar, a disciple of St. Columba.
Nigg —	The bay.
Peterculter —	Backland of the church dedicated to St. Peter.
Peterhead —	Headland of St. Peter's church.
Pitcaple —	Homestead of the mare.
Pitsligo —	Homestead abounding in shells.
Pitmedden —	Middle homestead.
Portgordon —	Built by the Duke of Richmond and Gordon in 1874.
Portknockie —	Harbour by the hillock.
Portsoy —	A good **or** safe harbour.
Rafford —	Village **or** fort on the height.
Rathen —	Said to be named after St. Ethernan, a former Bishop of Aberdeen, who consecrated several churches.
Rattray —	Fort dwelling **or** village.
Rhynie —	A point of land.
Rosehearty —	Place on the high headland **or** place of the dun coloured headland.
Rothes —	Place of the red water **or** fort dwelling.
Rothiemay —	Fort in the meadow **or** plain.
Ruthven —	Red rock **or** river.
Sauchen —	A muddy place **or** place of the willows.
Scurdargue —	Red pointed rock.
Shenval —	Old homestead.
Spittal of Glenmuck —	Hospice **or** hospital of the glen of the pig river.
Strathbogie —	Valley of the *sack* **or** *bag* river.
Strichen —	Valley of the Ugie **or** little water.
Succoth —	Point of land jutting out (literally *a snout).*

Tarland —	Level land **or** bull's enclosure.
Tarves —	Place of the bull.
Tomnaven —	Hillock of the river.
Tomintoul —	Hillock of the barn.
Tomnavoulin —	Hillock of the mill.
Torphins —	Clear **or** white hills **or** possibly named after Torfinn, a Scandinavian ally of Macbeth.
Torry —	Possibly, a mound **or** heap.
Tulloch —	The hillock.
Tullochs —	Hillocks.
Turriff —	Place of the tower.
Udny —	Probably, a little stream.
Ythanbank —	Bank of the *talking* river.

Aberarder —	Confluence of the high water.
Abriachan —	Confluence of the streamlet once called the Breachy.
Acharacle —	The ford **or** river of Torquil.
Achavanich —	Probably, field of the monk.
Achentoul —	Field of the barn.
Achgarve —	Rough field.
Achiemore —	Big field.
Achiltibuie —	Traditionally, the field of the yellow-haired boy. (This meaning is doubtful).
Achintee —	Field of the sudden attack **or** onrush.
Achmelvich —	Field of the sandbank bay.
Achnacarry —	Field of the weir.
Achnahanat —	Field of the mother church.
Achnaluachrach —	Field of the rushes.
Altlassmore —	Dwelling on the big steep bank.
Altnabreac —	Trout stream.
Altnaharra —	Stream of the fence **or** wall.
Alvie —	Island of swans **or** a rocky place.
Annat —	Mother church.
Applecross —	Mouth of the little cross.
Ardcharnich —	Height of the rocky ground.
Ardclach —	High stony ground.
Ardersier —	East point height.
Ardgay —	Height of the wind.
Ardgour —	Height of the goats.
Ardnamurchan —	Point of the great seas.
Ardochy —	High field.
Ardross —	Height of the moor.
Ardtornish —	Thori's headland.
Arisaid —	Bay of the river mouth.
Assynt —	Ridge **or** rock end.
Auchindrean —	Thorn field **or** field of strife.
Auchintoul —	Field of the barn.
Auchlunachan —	Field of the jointed grass.

Auchnashelloch –	Field of the willows.
Auchtascailt –	Field of the two bald places.
Auchtertyre –	Upper part of the land.
Auckingill –	Hakon's ravine, narrow glen.
Auldearn –	Stream of the Earn (probably the name of a local goddess).
Aultbea –	Birch stream.
Aultgrishan –	Probably, stream of the black and white water.
Aultvaich –	Stream of the byre.
Aviemore –	Big slope **or** hill face.
Badachro –	Grove **or** thicket of the sheep fold.
Badcall/Badcaul –	Hazel grove.
Badenoch –	Bushy place **or** drowned place (a reference to flooding by the River Spey).
Balblair –	Homestead of the plain.
Balchladdich –	Homestead of the shore, beach.
Balavil –	Homestead on the edge.
Balgowan –	Homestead of the smith.
Balintore –	Homestead of the dung field.
Balintraid –	Homestead by the shore.
Ballachullish –	Homestead on the strait, narrow channel.
Balchraggan –	Homestead of the rocky place.
Balloch –	Homestead by the loch.
Balmacaan –	Homestead of Cathan's sons.
Balmacara –	Homestead of Carra's sons.
Balnabruaich –	Homestead on the bank.
Balnacra –	Ford mouth of the cruives (salmon nets)
Balnagown –	Homestead of the smith.
Balnain –	Mouth of the little ford **or** homestead of the chapel.
Banavie –	Probably, pig's place.
Balnespick –	Homestead of the bishop.
Bealach nam Bo –	Pass of the cattle.
Beauly –	Beautiful place.
Belmaduthy –	Macduff's homestead.
Bettyhill –	Originally known as Bettyhill of Farr. It was founded about 1820 as a fishing

	and agricultural centre by Elizabeth, Countess of Sutherland.
Blairour —	Dun coloured plain.
Boat of Garten —	Named after the old ferry across the Spey. Garten = a little cornfield.
Bonar Bridge —	Bridge by the bottom ford, i.e. the lowest ford on the Kyle of Sutherland.
Borgue —	A stronghold.
Brabstermire —	Broad farm mire.
Braemore —	Large upland.
Brora —	Bridge river.
Bruan —	A bank **or** slope.
Bunacaimb —	Bottom of the meandering stream.
Bunchrew —	Foot of the trees.
Caithness —	Headland of the wild cats (an old tribal name).
Callert —	Hazel height.
Cambusmore —	Big bay.
Camusdarrach —	Bay of the oak trees.
Camusnagaul —	Bay of the stranger.
Cannich —	Probably named after the river of the same name and meaning *a sweet smelling shrub* **or** *standing water.*
Caol —	Narrow strait **or** channel.
Cawdor —	Hard water (reference to a stream name).
Clachnaharry —	Rock of watching, observation.
Clashmore —	Big narrow, shallow valley.
Clovulin —	Graveyard at the mill.
Clyth —	A hill slope **or** a hurdle **or** stockade to protect cattle.
Coigach —	Place of the fifths, i.e., one fifth of a davach — a reference to an old system of land measure.
Coignafearn —	Alderwood fifth (see Coigach).
Conchra —	Place of cruives (salmon nets).
Contin —	Confluence of the waters.
Convinth —	Free quartering, billeting — a reference to an old obligatory custom of providing hospitality for the king.

Corpach —	Place for corpses — possibly associated with nearby Annat (Mother church).
Corran —	Low cape tapering to a point.
Coylumbridge —	Bridge of the narrow leap.
Cromarty —	A crooked point **or** cape.
Culduie —	Place of the dark nook.
Cullicudden —	Creek of the cuddies (type of fish).
Culloden —	Place of the little pool.
Culrain —	Wood **or** nook of the ferns.
Diabaig —	Deep bay.
Dingwall —	Plain of assembly.
Dochfour —	A davach of pasture land (reference to an old system of land measure).
Dores —	Place by the waterside.
Dornie —	Stony **or** pebbly place.
Dornoch —	Stony **or** pebbly place.
Dorusduain —	Door **or** place of the dark water.
Dounreay —	Strong fort **or** fort **or** hill on the plain.
Drumbeg —	A little ridge.
Drumdyre —	Ridge of the grove.
Drumnadrochit —	Ridge of the bridge.
Drumochter —	The upper ridge.
Dulsie —	Meadow dwelling.
Duirinish —	Headland of the deer.
Dunbeath —	Hill **or** fort of the birch trees.
Dundonnell —	Originally, field of the two Donalds.
Durnamuck —	Pigs' grove.
Durness —	Black headland **or** headland of the deer.
Easter Fearn —	East village of the alder trees.
Edderton —	Between the forts, hills **or** dunes.
Erchless —	On the River Glass.
Eribol —	Homestead of the gravel beach.
Eskadale —	Ash dale.
Fain —	Bog channels.
Fasagrianach —	Dwelling by the rotten **or** withered tree.
Fasnakyle —	Resting place **or** dwelling by the wood.
Fassfern —	Resting place by the alder trees.

Fearn —	Alder trees.
Findon —	White **or** clear hillside.
Forse —	A waterfall.
Fort Augustus —	Named in 1716 after William Augustus, Duke of Cumberland.
Fort George —	Named in 1748 after George II.
Fortrose —	Under the headland.
Fort William —	Named about 1690 after William III.
Freswick —	Thrasi's bay (a Scandinavian personal name).
Gairloch —	Short loch.
Garve —	A rough place.
Gills —	A small narrow glen.
Glackour —	Place of the dun coloured narrow valley.
Glenborrodale —	Glen of the fortress.
Glencoe —	Narrow glen.
Glenelg —	Noble glen **or** glen of hunting **or** of the roe.
Glenn Finnan —	Named after St. Finnan, a contemporary of St. Columba.
Glengarry —	Glen of the rough river.
Glen Roy —	The red glen.
Gorstan —	Little corn field.
Grantown on Spey —	Founded in 1776 by Sir James Grant of Grant.
Guisachan —	Place of the pine wood.
Halcro —	Slope of the sheep fold.
Halkirk —	High church.
Helmsdale —	Hjalmund's dale.
Huna —	Huni's stream.
Inchkinloch —	Meadow at the end of the loch.
Inchlumpie —	Probably, a bare unfertile meadow.
Inchnadamph —	Meadow of the ox.
Inverailort —	Mouth of the snow shower loch.
Invercassley —	Confluence of the Cassley and Oykel rivers.
Inverdruie —	Confluence of the Druie and Spey rivers.
Invergordon —	Formerly called Inverbreckie **or** Inchbreky and renamed after Sir Alexander Gordon

	in the 18th century.
Inverkirkaig —	Mouth of the *church bay* river.
Inverlael —	Possibly, mouth of the muddy river **or** mouth of the river by the low hollow.
Invermoriston —	Mouth of the river of the big waterfall.
Inverness —	Mouth of the River Ness.
Inversanda —	Mouth of the sand water.
Invershiel —	Mouth of the flowing water.
Isauld —	Meadow by the stream.
John o'Groats —	Traditionally named after John de Groot, a Dutchman who settled in Caithness during the reign of James IV.
Kenmore —	Big head.
Kentallen —	Head of the little inlet.
Kentra —	Head of the beach **or** bay.
Keppoch —	Tillage plot.
Kessock Ferry —	Said to be named after the Irish monk St. Kessock **or** Kesog.
Kilbride —	Church of St. Bridget.
Kilcoy —	The nook **or** back of the wood.
Kildonan —	Church of St. Donan.
Killilan —	Church of St. Fillan.
Killundine —	Church of St. Fintan.
Kilmartin —	Church of St. Martin (of Tours).
Kilmorack —	Church of St. Moroc.
Kilmory —	Church of St. Mary **or** of St. Maelrubha.
Kilphedir —	Church of St. Peter.
Kiltarlity —	Church of St. Talorgain **or** Talarican.
Kiltearn —	Church of the Lord.
Kincardine —	Head of the thicket.
Kincraig —	Head of the rock.
Kingairloch —	Head of the short loch.
Kingussie —	Head of the pine wood.
Kinloch —	Head of the loch.
Kinlochbervie —	Head of the loch of the well **or** water.
Kinlocheil —	Head of the loch of the gleam of sunshine.
Kinlochewe —	Head of the loch of the cry **or** echo (Lòch Ewe was the old name of Loch Maree).

Kinloch Hourn —	Head of the loch of hell.
Kinlochleven —	Head of the loch of the elm trees.
Kinlochmoidart —	Head of the muddy sea loch.
Kinlochmore —	Head of the large loch.
Kintail —	Head of the salt water.
Knockan —	A little hillock.
Knockbain —	White **or** fair hillock.
Knoydart —	Possibly, Knut's sea loch.
Kyle of Lochalsh —	Strait of the fairy loch **or** loch of the rolling waves.
Kylesku —	A narrow strait.
Kylestome —	Strait of the headland.
Laggan —	A little hollow.
Laide —	Hillside **or** slope.
Larachbeg —	A small ruined building.
Latheron —	Hamlet of seals.
Ledgowan —	Smith's slope.
Letters —	Hill slopes.
Letterewe —	Hill slope of Loch Ewe (the old name of Loch Maree).
Letterfearn —	Slope of the alder tree.
Lettoch —	A half davach (reference to an old system of land measure).
Liddesdale —	Slope-dale.
Lochaber —	Loch of the marshes.
Lochdrum —	Loch of the ridge.
Lochinver —	Mouth of the loch.
Lochrosque —	Loch of the crossing.
Lybster —	Shelter place.
Mallaig —	Calm **or** placid bay.
Mallaigvaig —	Little Mallaig.
Mandally —	Small meadow **or** meadow of the kids.
Maryburgh —	Mary's town. Named after Queen Mary, wife of William III.
Mellon Charles —	Charles' little hill.
Melness —	Sandbank by the headland.
Melvaig —	Sandbank bay.
Melvich —	Sandbank bay.

Mey —	A plain.
Millbuie Forest —	Forest of the yellow bare hill.
Morangie Forest —	Forest of the big meadow **or** mound.
Morar —	Big water (a reference to the loch of the same name).
Morrich More —	A large sea plain.
Morvern —	Sea gap.
Morvich —	A sea plain.
Munlochy —	Foot of the loch.
Murkle —	Dark **or** murky place.
Nairn —	Formerly known as Invernairn, meaning mouth of the river of the alders **or** mouth of the submerging river.
Naust —	New dwelling.
Navidale —	Dale of the sanctuary.
Nybster —	New farm **or** farm on a rocky place.
Onich —	A frothy **or** foaming place.
Opinan —	A small bay.
Ormsaigbeg —	Ormi's little bay.
Ormsaigmore —	Ormi's big bay.
Plockton —	Lump town — a reference to the promontory on which it stands.
Polbain —	White hollow **or** pit.
Poolewe —	Deep water of Loch Ewe.
Porin —	Pasture place.
Portmahomack —	Port of St. Machalmac **or** Mocholmoy.
Portnancon —	Port of the dogs.
Ratagan —	Small fortified enclosure.
Reay —	A plain.
Rhynie —	A little fort.
Rosemarkie —	Probably, headland of the sailors.
Rothiemurchus —	Road **or** fort of the great pines.
Ruthven —	Red rock **or** red river.
Salen —	Sea pond.
Saltburn —	A reference to the days of the salt tax when this commodity was smuggled ashore and hidden in burns.
Sanachan —	Place of sorrel **or** a deer park.

Sanna —	Sand island.
Scatwell —	Field of tribute, i.e., a field for which tribute was paid to the king.
Scarfskerry —	Cormorant's rock.
Scrabster —	Skari's homestead **or** sea gull homestead.
Shieldaig —	Herring bay.
Strathan —	A small low lying valley.
Strath Bran —	Valley of the drizzle **or** valley of the raven (river name).
Strathkanaird —	Valley of the River Cainneart.
Strathpeffer —	Valley of the radiant **or** beautiful river.
Strome Ferry —	Ferry of the point **or** headland.
Strontian —	Point of the little hill. (We derive the word Strontium from this place name).
Struy —	A current **or** stream.
Tain —	Assembly place.
Thurso —	Bull river **or** Thor's river.
Tofts —	A group of homesteads.
Tombreck —	Speckled hillock.
Tomnahurich —	Hillock of the yew wood.
Torridon —	Place of portage. (A reference to the portage from the head of Loch Torridon through Glen Torridon to Loch Maree).
Torrisdale —	Thori's dale.
Toscaig —	A barrow strip.
Tarvie —	Bull's place.
Tullich —	The hillock.
Ullapool —	Possibly, Ulli's homestead.
Urray —	Possibly, new ford **or** fort on a projecting piece of land.
Wick —	A bay.

(11.) BUTE

Ardbeg —	Little headland.
Ascog —	River strip.
Kames —	A creek **or** bay.
Kerrycroy —	Hard **or** firm quarter.
Kilchattan —	Church of St. Cattan **or** Cathan.
Kingarth —	Head of the enclosure.
Port Bannatyne —	Named after a family called Bannachtyne.
Rothesay —	Meaning uncertain. Possibly, Rother's **or** Roderick's island.

(12.) ARRAN

Ballymichael —	Michael's homestead.
Brodick —	Broad bay.
Currie —	Circular glen **or** round hollow.
Dippin —	Twopenny-land.
Dougrie —	Dark glen.
Feorline —	Farthing-land.
Kildonan —	Church of St. Donan.
Kilmory —	Church of St. Mary.
Lagg —	A hollow.
Lamlash —	Isle of St. Molas.
Largybeg —	Place of small stones.
Lochranza —	Rowan water.
Sannox —	Sand bay.
Shiskine —	Marsh land.

(13.) ISLAY

Islay —	Meaning uncertain.
Ardbeg —	A little hieght or eminence.
Ardnahoe —	Height of the burial mound.
Ardnave —	Height or headland of the saints.
Bowmore —	Big house or cottage.
Bruichladdich —	Bank on the rocky shore or beach.
Bun an Uillt —	Foot or mouth of the stream.
Bunnahabhainn —	River mouth.
Cragabus —	Crook town.
Feolin Ferry —	Beach field ferry.
Gruinart —	Shallow sea loch (named after the loch).
Kiells —	Churches or burial places.
Kilchiaran —	Church of St. Ciaran.
Kilchoman —	Church of St. Coman.
Kildalton —	Church of the fosterling.
Killarrow —	Church of St. Maelrubha.
Kilmeny —	Possibly, church of the incantation or sign.
Lagavulin —	Hollow of the mill.
Laggan —	A little hollow.
Leckgruinart —	Flat stone or declivity by the shallow sea loch.
Oa (Mull of) —	Headland of the howe or cairn.
Octofad —	Long eighth, i.e., one eighth of a davach (reference to an old system of land measure).
Port Charlotte —	Named after Lady Charlotte, mother of W.F.Campbell of Islay.
Port Ellen —	Named in 1821 after Lady Ellenor, first wife of W ᴲ.Campbell of Islay.
Port na Haven —	Harbour of the river.

(14.) JURA

Jura —	Deer island **or** grove island.
Cabrach —	A grove **or** thicket.
Inverlussa —	Mouth of the river of herbs.
Keils —	Churches **or** burial places.
Lagg —	A hollow.
Lealt —	A half-burn, i.e., a burn **or** stream having a steep bank on one side.
Leargybreck —	Speckled slope.

(15.) MULL

Mull –	A promontory **or** headland.
Achlech –	Field of the flat stones.
Achnadrish –	Field of briars.
Ardachoil –	Point **or** headland of the wood.
Ardmeanach –	Middle headland.
Ardnacross –	Height of the cross.
Aridhglas –	Green hill pasture.
Aros –	River mouth.
Auchnacraig –	Field of the rock.
Bunessan –	Foot of the little waterfall.
Burg –	A fortress.
Calgary –	Kali's house **or** enclosure.
Craignure –	Rock of the yew tree.
Ensay –	Meadow island.
Fidden –	A green islet **or** piece of land left uncovered at high tide.
Fionnphort –	Blessed **or** holy harbour.
Gometra –	Godmund's island.
Kilfinichen –	Church of St. Findchan **or** Finan.
Killichronan –	Probably, church of St. Cronan.
Killunaig –	Church of St. Findoca.
Kilninian –	Church of St. Ninian.
Knock –	A hillock.
Lagganulva –	Ulf's little hollow.
Lettermore –	Big slope **or** hillside.
Mornish –	Narrow headland.
Pennyghael –	Penny-land of the Gael **or** Highlander.
Pennygown –	Penny-land of the smith.
Port na Curaich –	Port **or** haven of the coracle – the supposed landing place of St. Columba on Iona in 563.
Quinish –	Headland of the cattle enclosure.
Ross of Mull –	Mull peninsula.
Salen –	Little inlet **or** arm of the sea.
Torbermory –	Well of Mary.
Ulva –	Ulf's island **or** wolf island.

Iona — The meaning is uncertain as the present spelling is believed to be the result of a scribe's error. However, tradition states that the name means simply *The Island* or (using a fuller Gaelic version) *The Island of the cell or church of Columba).*

(16.) TIREE

Tiree —	Probably, land of corn.
Balephetrish —	Peter's homestead.
Balephuil —	Homestead by the pool.
Ballevullin —	Homestead of the mill.
Barradhu —	Black height **or** point.
Scarinish —	Headland of the young sea-gull.

(17.) ISLE OF SKYE

(including its offshore islands)

Skye —	The *Winged Isle.* (traditional meaning) **or** the island of cloud **or** the *cut* **or** *indented* island. (a reference to the coastline)
The Aird —	The headland.
Ardvasar —	Fatal headland.
Armadale —	Dale of the bay.
Arnisort —	Arni's sea loch.
Bachandroman —	Probably, cow house of the ridge.
Balgowan —	Homestead of the smith.
Balnaknock —	Homestead by the hillock.
Bracadale —	Dale with a steep slope.
Breakish —	Place of the slope.
Broadford —	Broad firth **or** sea inlet.
Calligarry —	Kali's house **or** enclosure.
Camastianavaig —	Probably, sheltered bay **or** creek.
Carbost —	Homestead by the copse.
Digg —	A ditch **or** mound (to keep out the water).
Drumfearn —	Ridge of the alder trees.
Drynoch —	Place abounding in thorns.
Duisdale —	Misty **or** gloomy dale.
Dunan —	Little hill **or** fort.
Duntulm —	Hillock of the islet.
Dunvegan —	Began's fort.
Edinbain —	Fair hill-face.
Eilean Heast —	Horse island.
Fiskavaig —	Fish bay.
Greshornish —	Headland of the pig.
Hallin —	Place by the slope.
Husabost —	Homestead of the house.
Isle Ornsay —	Ebb-tide island.
Kensaleyre —	Head of the sea by the gravel beach.
Kilbride —	Church of St. Bridget.
Kilmaluag —	Church of St. Moluag.

Kilmarie —	Church of St. Maelrubha.
Kilmuir —	Church of St. Mary.
Kilvaxter —	Thought to be the *Church of the baker*, i.e., one who baked bread for the monastery at nearby Monkstadt.
Kirkibost —	Homestead by the church.
Knock —	A hillock.
Kyle Akin —	Strait **or** narrow channel of Hakon (a Norwegian king).
Kyle Rhea —	Strait **or** narrow channel of the king.
Lephin —	Halfpenny-land.
Lincro —	Meadow of the fold.
Luib —	A bend.
Minginish —	Big headland.
Ollach —	Rank grass.
Orbost —	Orri's homestead.
Ord —	A round steep mountain.
Pabay —	Priest's island.
Peinchorran —	Penny-land of the low cape.
Peinlick —	Penny-land of the doctor.
Penfiler —	Penny-land of the fiddler.
Portree —	King's harbour (commemorates a visit by James V in 1540).
Raasay —	Possibly, roe ridge island.
Rona —	Hill of rough ground.
Scalpay —	Boat-shaped island.
Skulamus —	Skuli's moss **or** moorland.
Skeabost —	Skidi's homestead.
Sleat —	Flat piece of land.
Soay —	Sheep island.
Staffin —	Place of pillars, i.e., basaltic rock.
Stein —	A stone.
Stenscoll —	Stony slope.
Talisker —	A sloping rock.
Tarskavaig —	Cod bay.
Teangue —	A tongue **or** spit of land.
Tókavaig —	Hawk bay.
Trotternish —	Possibly, Throndar's headland.
Uig —	A bay **or** creek.
Vaternish —	Water headland.

Achmore —	Big field.
Aignish —	Ridge point.
Aird Fenish —	Headland of the sheep.
Aird Tunga —	A tongue **or** spit of land.
Arnish —	Ari's headland.
Balallan —	Homestead of the meadow.
Balranald —	Ronald's homestead.
Barra —	Island of St. Barr **or** Findbarr.
Barvas —	A fort.
Bayble —	Priest's town.
Benbecula —	Traditionally, mountain of the fords.
Bernera —	Bjorn's island.
Bornish —	Headland of the fort.
Bratanish —	Steep headland.
Breasclete —	Broad ridge **or** cliff.
Brenish —	Broad headland.
Brue —	A bridge.
Callanish/Callernish —	Headland of Kali **or** Kjallar (a Norse name for Odin).
Carinish —	Kari's headland.
Carloway —	Karl's bay.
Coilleag a'Phrionsa —	Prince's bay.
Coll —	A summit.
Earshader —	Beach homestead.
Enaclete —	Brow cliff.
Eoropie —	Beach town.
Eriskay —	Erik's island.
Garrynahine —	Enclosure of the river.
Grimanish —	Grim's headland.
Grimshader —	Grim's homestead.
Habost —	High homestead.
Islivig —	Ice slope bay.
Kilpheder —	Church of St. Peter.
Kiriwick —	Quiet bay.
Kirkibost —	Church homestead.
Laxay —	Salmon water.
Laxdale —	Salmon river dale.

Leurbost —	Clay homestead.
Leverburgh —	Named after Lord Leverhulme who set up a fishing station here.
Lingay —	Heather island.
Mealasta —	Sandbank homestead.
Melbost —	Sandbank homestead.
Miavaig —	Narrow bay.
Orosay/Orinsay —	Ebb tide island.
Pabbay —	Priest's island.
Shawbost —	Homestead by the sea.
Shulishader —	Pillar homestead.
Soval —	Sheep hill.
Stornoway —	Meaning uncertain: star bay **or** rudder bay.
Swanibost —	Sweyn's homestead.
Swordale —	Grassy dale.
Tolsta —	Tholf's homestead.
Tolstachaolais —	The strait by Tholf's homestead.
Uachdar —	Upper part **or** upland.
Uig —	A bay.
Uist —	An abode.
Vatisker Point —	Point of the isolated rock in the sea.

Orkney —	Probably, whale island.
Burray —	Fortress **or** broch island.
Burwick —	Fortress **or** broch bay.
Cleat —	Rocky eminence.
Eday —	Isthmus island.
Egilsay —	Egill's island.
Flotta —	Fleet island.
Georth —	Farm settlement.
Grimbister —	Grim's homestead.
Hobbister —	Homestead by the mound.
Hoy —	High island.
Kirkwall —	Church bay.
Longhope —	Long bay.
Midbea —	Middle farm.
Orgill —	Ravine of the stream.
Orphir —	Ebb-tide island.
Papa Stour —	Great Priest's island.
Papa Westray —	Priest's western island.
Rousay —	Rolf's island.
Sanday —	Sandy island.
Scapa —	Boat-shaped island.
Shapinsay —	Helping island. (So called because of its convenient location for seamen.)
St. Margaret's Hope —	St. Margaret's Bay.
Stromness —	Headland of the stream **or** current.
Stronsay —	Probably, profitable island.
Swanbister —	Probably, Sveinn's homestead.
Toab —	Probably, toll bay.
Tressness —	Possibly, Thrasi's headland.
Westray —	Western island.
Walls —	Place of bays.
Wyre —	Spearhead.

(20.) SHETLAND ISLANDS

Shetland —	Probably, land shaped like a sword.
Breibister —	Broad homestead.
Brough —	A fortress **or** broch.
Burravoe —	Fortress bay.
Dalsetter —	Homestead of the valley.
Hamnavo —	Bay of the harbour.
Isbister —	Homestead towards the east.
Kirkabister —	Homestead by the church.
Lambhoga Head —	Lamb's pasture head.
Laxa —	Salmon water.
Lerwick —	Mud bay.
Muckle Flugga —	Big precipices.
Otterswick —	Ottar's bay.
Scalloway —	Bay of the huts **or** cottages.
Skellister —	Skjolder's homestead.
Tingwall —	Plain of assembly.
Tolob —	Probably, toll bay.
Uyea —	Flat fertile land by the water.
Whalsay —	Whale island.
Yell —	Barren island.

MISCELLANEOUS ISLANDS

Canna –	Probably, porpoise island.
Coll –	Traditionally, a harbour.
Colonsay –	Probably, hazel island.
Cumbrae (Great/ Little) –	Island of the Cumbrians **or** Welsh.
Danna –	Dane's island.
Eigg –	Island of the notch **or** ridge.
Fair Isle –	Sheep island.
Foula –	Bird island.
Gigha –	God's island.
Handa –	Sand island.
Inchcolm –	St. Columba's island.
Inchmarnock –	St. Marnoc's island.
May –	Gull island.
Muck –	Pig island.
Oran/Oransay –	Ebb-tide island.
Scarba –	Cormorant island.
Seil –	Seal island.
Shuna –	Scouting island.
Staffa –	Pillar island.
Stroma –	Island of the stream **or** current.
Tanera More –	Big harbour island.
Eileach an Naoimh –	Island of the saint.
Eilean Dubh Mor –	Big black island.
Garbh Eileach –	Rough rocky island.

LOCHS

Achall —	Probably, loch of the field of calamity **or** loss.
Achray —	Meaning uncertain, but possibly, loch of the churning water **or** loch of the level field **or** loch of the field of devotion.
Affric —	Loch of the speckled water.
Ailort —	Loch of the snow showers.
Ainort —	Eyvind's **or** Einar's sea loch.
Aline —	Beautiful loch.
Ard —	High loch.
Arklet —	Possibly, loch of the difficult slope.
Assynt —	Loch of the rock end.
Avich —	Water loch.
Avon —	Loch of the river **or** the very bright loch.
Awe —	Water loch.
Beannacharan —	Probably, the pointed **or** peaked loch.
Beinn a' mheadhoin —	Loch of the middle mountain.
A'Bhealaich —	Loch of the pass **or** gap.
A'Bhraoin —	Loch of the rain **or** showers.
Breivat —	Broadwater loch.
Broom —	Loch of the rain **or** showers.
Buie —	Yellow loch.
Caolisport —	Loch of the port by the strait.
Carron —	Loch of the rough **or** stony river.
A'Chairn Bhain —	Loch of the white cairn.
Choire —	Loch of the corrie **or** circular glen.
Chon —	Loch of the dogs.
A'Chroisg —	Loch of the crossing.
Clair —	Loch of the level place.
Cluanie —	Loch of the green pastures.
Coruisk —	Loch of the circular glen of the waters.
Coultrie —	Loch of the narrow place.
Creran —	Probably, loch of the tree.
Diabaig —	Deep bay loch.
Druim a'chliabhain —	Loch of the ridge of the creel **or** hamper.

Dughaill —	Dugald's loch.
Duich —	Loch of St. Duthac.
Earn —	Possibly, west loch **or** loch of Ireland.
Eck —	Probably, water loch.
Eil —	Loch of the gleam of sunshsine.
Eishort —	Sea loch of the isthmus.
Eriboll —	Loch of the homestead by the gravel beach.
Erisort —	Eric's sea loch.
Etive —	Loch of the cattle (traditional meaning) **or** the horrid loch.
Ewe —	Loch of the cry **or** echo.
Eye —	Loch of the isthmus.
Fada (Lochan) —	Long little loch.
An Fhirbhallaich —	Loch of the trout.
Finlaggan —	Loch of St. Finluga **or** Finlagan (a contemporary of St. Columba).
Frisa —	Loch of the freezing water.
Fyne —	Middle **or** white loch.
Gairloch —	Short loch.
Garry —	Loch of the rough water **or** loch of the garden **or** enclosure.
Garve —	Rough loch.
Gilp —	Chisel loch.
Glass —	Grey loch **or** water loch.
Glascarnoch —	Loch of the grey stony ground **or** loch of the cleft **or** ditch in the stony ground.
Glendhu —	Loch of the black glen.
Goil —	The raging **or** boiling loch **or** the forked loch.
Greshornish —	Loch of the pigs' headland.
Gruinart —	Shallow sea loch.
Grunavat —	Green loch.
Hope —	Loch of the bay.
Hourn —	Loch of hell (traditional meaning) **or** loch of the berry gap (possible alternative).

Inchard —	Loch of the height of the ash trees **or** loch of the meadow height.
Indaal —	Loch of the division.
Katrine —	Meaning uncertain. May contain an element meaning *battle* **or** *wood* **or** *dark*.
Kishorn —	Probably, loch of the large headland.
Laggan —	Loch of the little hollow.
Langavat —	Long water loch.
Laxavat —	Loch of the salmon water.
Laxford —	Sea loch of the salmon.
Leven —	Loch of the elm trees.
Linnhe —	Loch of the pool.
Lochy —	Black loch.
Lomond —	Loch of Ben Lomond (Beacon Mountain) **or** loch of the elm trees.
Long —	Loch of the ships.
Loyal —	Loch of the law field.
Loyne —	Loch of beauty **or** loch of the swampy plain.
Lubnaig —	Crooked loch.
Luichart —	Loch of the camp **or** refuge.
Lyon —	Loch of the elm trees **or** loch of the flood river.
Maddy —	Loch of the dogs.
Maree —	Loch of St. Maelrubha.
Meadie —	Possibly, loch of the increase.
Melfort —	Loch of the sand dune bay.
Merkland —	Loch of the markland (reference to an old system of land measure).
Moidart —	Probably, muddy sea loch.
Monar —	Possibly, loch of the high land.
Morar -	Big water loch.
More —	Big loch.
Morie —	Probably, loch of St. Mary.
Mullardoch —	Loch of the high bare hill.
Nagar —	Loch of the goats.
Nell —	Loch of the swans.
Ness —	Loch of the River Ness. (Ness may mean *wet* or *water* and may also have been the name of an ancient Celtic river goddess).

73

Nevis —	Loch of heaven (traditional meaning) **or** the venemous loch (possible alternative).
Oich —	Loch of the water place.
Na h-oidhche —	Loch of the night.
Orrin —	Loch of the offering **or** loch of the beech tree.
Ossian —	Loch of Ossian (a legendary warrior and poet).
Quoich —	Loch of the cup. (So named from the shape of the surrounding land).
Rannoch —	Fern loch.
Ranza —	Loch of the rowan tree.
An Ruathair —	Loch of the sudden violence.
Na Scaravat —	Loch of the young sea gull.
Seaforth —	Loch of the narrow sea inlet.
Na Sealga —	Loch of the hunting, fowling.
Shiel —	Possibly, loch of the flowing water.
Shin —	Loch of the charm.
Sloy —	Loch of the host **or** multitude.
Snizort —	Sea loch of the snow.
Stack —	Loch of the stack shaped mountain.
Strandavat —	Loch of the strand water.
Striven —	Loch of strife.
Sween —	Sweyn's loch (associated with the MacSweens).
Tamanavay —	Loch of the harbour bay.
Tarsan —	The oblique loch.
Tay —	The quiet **or** silent loch.
Torridon —	Loch of the place of portage.
Treig —	Loch of desolation.
Tuath —	North loch.
Tummel —	The dark **or** gloomy loch.
Nan Uamh —	Loch of the caves.
Uskavagh —	Loch of the bay of the water.
Vaich —	Loch of the byre.
Venachar —	Probably, the ointed **or** peaked loch.
Veyatie —	Possibly, loch of despondency.
Voil —	The fervent **or** active loch.
Watten —	Water loch.

BEINN (anglicised as **BEN**) usually applies to a large high mountain standing by itself.

Beinn nan Aighenan —	Possibly, mountain of the shallow pans.
Beinn Aird Da Loch —	Mountain height of two lochs **or** mountain between two lochs.
Beinn nam Ban —	Mountain of the women.
Beinn nam Beathrach —	Mountain of the wild beasts **or** mountain of the thunderbolts.
Beinn Bhalgairean —	Mountain of the foxes.
Beinn Bhan —	The white **or** fair mountain.
Beinn Bharrain —	Mountain top.
Beinn Bheag —	Small mountain.
Beinn a'Bheithir —	Mountain of the wild beast **or** mountain of the thunderbolt.
Beinn Bhuidhe —	Yellow mountain.
Beinn a'Bhuiridh —	Mountain of the roaring deer.
Beinn a'Bhutha —	Mountain of the hut **or** cottage.
Beinn Bhreac —	Speckled mountain.
Beinn na Caillich —	Mountain of the old woman.
Beinn nan Caorach —	Mountain of the sheep.
Beinn nan Carn —	Mountain of the cairns.
Beinn a'Chaisteal —	Mountain of the castle.
Beinn Chaorach —	Mountain of the sheep.
Beinn a'Chapaill —	Mountain of the mare **or** horse.
Beinn Chapull —	Mountain of the mare **or** horse.
Beinn Cheathaich —	Mountain of the mist.
Beinn a'Chlachair —	Mountain of the stonemason.
Beinn Chreagach —	Rocky mountain.
Beinn a'Chroinn —	Mountain of the plough **or** mountain of the tree.
Beinn a'Chuirn —	Mountain of the cairn.
Beinn na Cille —	Mountain of the church **or** burial place.
Beinn na Croise —	Mountain of the cross.
Beinn Damh —	Mountain of the stag.
Beinn Dearg —	Red mountain.
Beinn Dhorain —	Mountain of the otter **or**

	mountain of the *little water*.
Beinn Doran —	Mountain of the otter **or** mountain of the little water.
Beinn an Dothaidh —	Mountain of the scorching.
Beinn Dronaig —	Mountain of the ridge **or** hump.
Beinn na Duathrach —	Mountain of darkness.
Beinn Dubhchraig —	Mountain of the black rock.
Beinn Eighe —	File mountain.
Beinn Eilideach —	Mountain of the roe deer.
Beinn an Eoin —	Mountain of the bird.
Beinn nan Eun —	Mountain of the birds.
Beinn Eunaich —	Mountain of the fowl.
Beinn Fhada —	Long mountain.
Beinn Fhionnlaidh —	Finlay's mountain.
Beinn Fhogharaidh —	Mountain of the harvest **or** crop.
Beinn Ghlas —	Green **or** grey mountain.
Beinn a'Ghlo —	Mountain of mist.
Beinn Ghobhlach —	Forked mountain.
Beinn na Gulaig —	Probably, mountain of lamentation.
Beinn Ime —	Mountain of butter.
Beinn Iutharn Bheag —	Little mountain of hell.
Beinn Iutharn Mhor —	Big mountain of hell.
Beinn Leabhainn —	Mountain of the elm trees.
Beinn Leoid —	Mountain of the expanse **or** breadth.
Beinn Liath Mhor —	Big grey mountain.
Beinn Liath Mhor a'Ghiubhas Li —	Big grey mountain of the coloured pine.
Beinn na Lice —	Mountain of the flat stone.
Beinn nan Lus —	Mountain of the plants **or** herbs.
Beinn a'Mheadhoin —	Middle mountain.
Beinn Mheadoin —	Middle mountain.
Beinn Mheadhonach —	Middle mountain.
Beinn Mholach —	Rough, stormy mountain.
Beinn Odhar —	Dun coloured mountain.
Beinn Odhar Bheag —	Small dun mountain.
Beinn an Oir —	Mountain of the gold.
Beinn nan Ramh —	Mountain of the wood.
Beinn an Rubha Riabhach —	Mountain of the grey point **or** headland.

Beinn na Seilg —	Mountain of hunting.
Beinn Shiantaidh —	Stormy mountain.
Beinn an t-Sneachda —	Mountain of the snow.
Beinn Spionnaidh —	Mountain of force **or** strength.
Beinn na Sroine —	Mountain of the point.
Beinn Starav —	Stout **or** robust mountain.
Beinn Suidhe —	Mountain of the seat.
Beinn Tarsuinn —	Oblique mountain.
Beinn Trilleachain —	Mountain of the grey plover.
Beinn an Tuirc —	Mountain of the wild boar.
Beinn Tulaichean —	Mountain of the hillock.
Beinn Uidhe —	Mountain of the slow moving water.
Beinn Uraraidh —	Verdant **or** blooming mountain.
Ben Attow —	Long mountain.
Ben Armine —	Mountain of the chief **or** hero.
Ben Alder —	Mountain of the water of the steep rocks.
Ben Alisky —	Mountain of the water of the steep rocks.
Ben Bhuidhe Mor —	Big yellow mountain.
Ben Challum —	Malcolm's mountain.
Ben Cruachan —	Mountain of the rounded peak.
Ben Griam Beg —	Small lichen mountain.
Ben Griam More —	Big lichen mountain.
Ben Hee —	Mountain of peace.
Ben Hiant —	Holy mountain.
Ben Hope —	Mountain of the bay.
Ben Klibreck —	Mountain of the cliff slope.
Ben Lawers —	Echoing mountain.
Ben Lomond —	Mountain of the beacon **or** mountain of Loch Lomond (loch of the elm trees).
Ben Loyal —	Mountain of the law field.
Ben Lui —	Mountain of the calf.
Ben Macdui (Macdhui) —	Mountain of the black pig **or** MacDuff's mountain.
Ben More —	Big mountain.
Ben More Assynt —	Big mountain of the rock end.
Ben More Coigach —	Big mountain of the place of the fifths (reference to an old system of land measure).

Ben Nevis —	Mountain of heaven (traditional meaning) **or** the venomous mountain.
Ben Stack —	Stack mountain.
Ben Tee —	Fairy mountain.
Ben Venue —	Small mountain.
Ben Vrackie —	Speckled mountain.
Ben Vuirich —	Mountain of the roaring **or** bellowing.
Ben Wyvis —	Majestic mountain **or** terrible mountain.
Ard Bheinn —	Top of the mountain.
Baos Bheinn —	Capricious mountain.
Chruinn Bheinn —	Round mountain.
Crois Bheinn —	Cross mountain.
Dubh Bheinn —	Black mountain.
Fionn Bheinn —	White mountain.
Fuar Bheinn —	Cold mountain.
Garbh Bheinn —	Rough mountain.
Glais Bheinn —	Green **or** grey mountain.
Glas Bheinn —	Green **or** grey mountain.
Ladhar Bheinn —	Forked mountain.
Meith Bheinn —	Fat mountain.
Mor Bheinn —	Big mountain.

CARN: usually a mountain standing by itself but covered with rocks and stones.

Carn Allt a'Chlaiginn —	Cairn of the skull stream.
Carn Aosda —	Old cairn.
Carn Ban —	White cairn.
Carn Ban Mor —	Big white cairn.
Carn Beag —	Small cairn.
Carn Beag Dearg —	Small red cairn.
Carn a'Bhiorain —	Cairn of the stick **or** staff.
Cairn Breac —	Speckled cairn.
Carn a'Chaochain —	Cairn of the rivulet.
Carn a'Choin Deirg —	Cairn of the red dog.
Carn a'Choire —	Cairn of the round hollow.
Carn a'Chuillin —	Cairn of the holly.
Carn Chuinneag —	Cairn of the bucket **or** water-spout.

Carn na Coinnich —	Cairn of the moss.
Carn Coire na Creiche —	Cairn of the round hollow of the plunder or devastation.
Carn a'Choire Mhoir —	Cairn of the big round hollow.
Carn an Daimh Bhain —	Cairn of the white stag.
Carn Dearg —	Red Cairn.
Carn Dearg Mor —	Big red cairn.
Carn na Drochaide —	Cairn of the bridge.
Carn na Dubh Choille —	Cairn of the black wood.
Carn Dubh 'Ic an Deoir —	MacIndeoir's black cairn.
Carn Eige —	Cairn of the notch or gap.
Carn Eiteige —	Cairn of the white stone or quartz.
Carn an Fhreidceadain —	Cairn of the sentinel or guard.
Carn na Fiacail —	Cairn of the tooth.
Carn nam Fiaclan —	Cairn of the teeth.
Carn nan Gabhar/ Gobhar —	Cairn of the goats.
Carn a'Gheoidh —	Cairn of the goose.
Carn Ghiubhais —	Cairn of the fir tree.
Carn Ghlas Choire —	Cairn of the green round hollow.
Carn Ghlinne —	Cairn of the glen.
Carn a'Ghobhair —	Cairn of the goat.
Cairngorm —	Blue cairn.
Carn nan Iomairean —	Cairn of the unploughed ridges.
Carn Leac —	Cairn of the flat stone.
Carn Liath —	Grey cairn.
Carn Loch na Gobhlag —	Cairn of the fork loch.
Carn Mhic an Toisich —	MacIntosh's cairn.
Carn Mor Dearg —	Big red cairn.
Carn Odhar —	Dun coloured cairn.
Carn an Righ —	King's cairn.
Carn Salachaidh —	Cairn of the filth or defilement.
Carn na Saobhaidh(e) —	Cairn of the wild beast's den.
Carn an t-Sean-Liathanach —	Cairn of the grey old man.

Carn Sgulain —	Cairn of the little old man.
Carn Sleumhuinn —	Slippery cairn.
Carn an t-Suidhe —	Cairn of the seat (i.e., natural level shelf).
Cairntaggart —	Cairn of the priest.
Cairntoul —	Cairn of the barn.
Carn nan Tri-Tighearnan —	Cairn of the three masters **or** rulers.
Carn an Tuirc —	Cairn of the wild boar.
Geal Charn —	White cairn.
Geal Charn Mor —	Big white cairn.

CNOC (sometimes pronounced **CROC**): A knoll **or** hillock.

Cnoc Breac —	Speckled hillock.
Cnoc a'Chapuill —	Hillock of the mare **or** horse.
Cnoc a'Choire —	Hillock of the round hollow.
Cnoc Coinnich —	Mossy hillock.
Cnoc na Craobh —	Hillock of the tree.
Cnoc Dubh —	Black hillock.
Cnoc an Ime —	Hillock of the butter.
Cnoc a'Mhadaidh —	Hillock of the wolf **or** dog.
Cnoc Reamhar —	Big hillock.

CREAG: A Rock.

Creag Bhreac —	Speckled rock.
Creag na Criche —	Boundary rock.
Creag a'Chaoruinn —	Rock of the rowan tree.
Creag Dubh —	Black rock.
Creag an Dubh Loch —	Rock of the black loch.
Creag Dhubh Mhor —	Big black rock.
Creag na h-Eige —	Rock of the notch **or** gap.
Creag na Fhithich —	Rock of the raven.
Creag nan Clachan Geala —	Rock of the white stones.
Creag nan Gall —	Rock of the strangers.
Creag Ghlas Laggan —	Grey rock of the little hollow.
Creag a'Ghlas—Uillt —	Rock of the grey stream.

Creag Leacach —	Rock with large flat stones.
Creag an Leth-Choin —	Rock of the lurcher (kind of hunting dog).
Creag a'Mhaim —	Rock of the large round hill **or** rock of the mountain pass.
Creag Mhor —	Big rock.
Creag nam Mial —	Rock of the lice.
Creag Rainich —	Fern rock.
Creag Ruadh —	Red rock.
Creag an t-Sithein —	Rock of the little hill.
Creag an Tarmachain —	Rock of the ptarmigan.
Creag Toll a'Choin —	Rock of the dog's hollow.
Creag Uchdag —	Steep rock.

CRUACH: A bold round hill standing apart.

A'Chruach —	The round hill top.
Cruach Ardrain —	Hill of the roar **or** shriek.
Cruach Bhreac-Liath —	Grey speckled hill.
Cruach na Capull —	Hill of the mares **or** horses.
Cruach Chuilceachan —	Hill abounding in reeds.
Cruachan Dearg —	Small red hill.
Cruach an Eachlaich —	Hill of the groom.
Cruach nam Fearna —	Hill of the alder trees.
Cruach nan Gabhar —	Hill of the goats.
Cruach an Lochain —	Hill of the little loch.
Cruach Lusach —	Hill abounding in herbs **or** plants.
Cruach Maolachy —	Hill becoming bare on top.
Cruach Mhic Fhionnlaidh —	Finlayson's hill.
Cruach Mhor —	Big round hill.
Cruach Neuran —	Hill of the sapling.
Cruach a'Phubuill —	Hill of the tent **or** pavilion.
Cruach an Tailleir —	Hill of the tailor.
Cruach an Uillt Fhearna —	Hill of the alder stream.

MEALL: A large rounded hill.

Am Meallan —	The little hill.
Meall nan Aighean —	Hill of the heifers.
Meall na h-Aistre —	Hill of the abode.
Meall Ban —	White hill.
Meall Bhenneit —	Bennet's hill.
Meall a'Bhuachaille —	Hill of the shepherd **or** herdsman.
Meall a'Bhuiridh —	Hill of the roaring deer.
Meall Blair —	Hill of the plain.
Meall nam Bradhan —	Hill of the salmon.
Meall Buidhe —	Yellow hill.
Meall a'Chaoruinn —	Hill of the rowan tree.
Meall a'Chathaidh —	Hill of the drifting snow **or** hill of the winnowing.
Meall a'Choire Bhuidhe —	Hill of the yellow hollow.
Meall a'Choire Leith —	Hill of the grey hollow.
Meall a'Chrasgaidh —	Hill of the box **or** coffer.
Meall Chuaich —	Hill of the cup shaped hollow.
Meall a'Churain —	Hill of the brave man.
Meall nan Con —	Hill of the dogs.
Meall Cuanail —	Hill of the band of singers **or** hill of the flocks.
Meall nan Damh —	Hill of the stags.
Meall an Damhain —	Hill of the spider.
Meall Dearg —	Red hill.
Meall Dearg Choire nam Muc —	Red hill of the hollow of the pigs.
Meall Dubh —	Black hill.
Meall an Fheur Lock —	Hill of the reedy loch **or** swamp.
Meall nam Fiadh —	Hill of the deer.
Meall nam Fuaran —	Hill of the well **or** spring.
Mealfourvonie —	Hill of the cold moor.
Meall Gaothair —	Windy hill.
Meall Garbh —	Rough hill.
Meall Ghlas —	Green hill.
Meall a'Ghrianain —	Hill with the sunny top.
Meall na Leitrach —	Hill with the broad slope.

Meall Liath Choire —	Grey hill of the round hollow.
Meall Luaidhe —	Hill of the lead.
Meall Meadhonach —	Middle hill.
Meall Mhic Iomhair —	MacIver's hill.
Meall a'Mhuic —	Hill of the pig.
Meall Mor —	Big hill.
Meall Odhar —	Dun coloured hill.
Meall a'Phubuill —	Hill of the tent **or** pavilion.
Meall Reamhar —	Thick round hill.
Meall an Seallaidh —	Hill with a wide view.
Meall nan Tarmachan —	Hill of the ptarmigan.
Meall an Tuirc —	Hill of the wild boar.
Meall nan Uan —	Hill of the lambs.
Meallach Mhor —	Big round lumpy hill.
Meallan Liath Coire Mhic Dhugaill —	Grey hill of MacDougal's round hollow.
Meallan Liath Mor —	Big grey hillock.
Ruadh Mheall —	Red coloured hill.

SGURR, SGOR: A high, circular, sharp pointed peak standing by itself, or a steep height on another mountain.

Sgurr na h-Aide —	Peak of the hat.
Sgurr an Airgid —	Peak of silver.
Sgurr Alasdair —	Alistair's peak.
Sgurr na Ba Glaise —	Peak of the grey cow.
Sgurr a'Bhealaich Dheirg —	Peak of the red gap **or** pass.
Sgurr nan Ceathreamhnan —	Peak of the quarters **or** lodgings. (The quarters may refer to an old system of land measure).
Sgurr Choinnich —	Mossy peak.
Sgurr a'Choire Ghlais —	Peak of the green **or** grey hollow.
Sgurr na Ciste Ghlais —	Peak of the black chest.
Sgurr nan Coireachan —	Peak of the rounded hollows.
Sgurr nan Conbhairean —	Peak of the dog men.
Sgurr/Sgorr Dhearg —	Red peak.

Sgurr Dhomnuill –	Donald's peak.
Sgurr Dhomnuill Mor –	Big Donald's peak.
Sgor na Diollaid –	Peak of the saddle.
Sgurr na h-Eachainne –	Peak of the brains **or** ingenuity.
Sgurr nan Eag –	Peak of the notches **or** gaps.
Sgurr nan Eugallt –	Possibly, peak of the death streams.
Sgorr nam Faoileann –	Peak of the seagulls.
Sgurr Fhuaran –	Peak of the well **or** spring.
Sgurr Fhuar-Thuill –	Peak of the cold hollow.
Sgor Gaibhre –	Peak of the goat.
Sgor Gaoith –	Peak of the wind.
Sgurr Ghiubhsachain –	Peak of the little pine wood.
Sgurr a'Ghreadaidh –	Peak of the winnowing.
Sgurr nan Gillean –	Peak of the young men.
Sgurr na Lapaich –	Peak of the swamp or bog.
Sgurr an Lochain –	Peak of the little loch.
Sgurr a'Mhadaidh –	Peak of the wolf **or** dog.
Sgurr a'Mhaoraich –	Peak of the shell fish.
Sgurr Mhic Coinnich –	MacKenzie's peak.
Sgurr Mhor –	Big peak.
Sgurr a'Mhuillin –	Peak of the mill.
Sgurr Mor –	Big peak.
Sgurr na Moraich –	Peak of the sea plain.
Sgurr na Muice –	Peak of the pig.
Sgurr na Ruaidhe –	Peak of the red deer.
Sgurr nan Saighead –	Peak of the arrows.
Sgurr Thearlaich –	Charles' peak.
Sgurr Thuilm –	Peak of the round hillock.
Sgor na h-Ulaidh –	Peak of the treasure.

STOB: A peak **or** point.

Stob an Aonaich Mhoir –	Point of the big ridge **or** height.
Stob a'Bhruaich Leith –	Point of the grey bank.
Stob Binnein –	Hill with a pointed top.
Stob na Broige –	Peak of the shoe.
Stob a'Choin –	Peak of the dog.

Stob na Cruaiche —	Peak of the round hill.
Stob Dearg —	Red point.
Stob na Doire —	Peak of the grove **or** thicket.
Peak an Fhir-Bhogha —	Peak of the archer.
Stob Garbh —	Rough point.
Stob Ghabhar —	Goat point.
Stob a'Ghrianan —	Sunshine peak.
Stob Mhic Bheathain —	MacBain's peak.
Stob an t-Sluichd —	Peak of the hollow **or** pit.
Stob Coir an Albannaich —	Peak of the round hollow of the Scotsman.
Stob Coire nam Beith —	Peak of the round hollow of the beech trees.
Stob Coire Bhealaich —	Peak of the round hollow of the pass **or** gap.
Stob Coire Cath na Sine —	Peak of the round hollow of the battle of the elements.
Stob Coire a'Chairn —	Peak of the round hollow of the cairn.
Stob Coire a'Chearcaill —	Peak of the round hollow of the circle.
Stob Coire Dheirg —	Peak of the red round hollow.
Stob Coire Dhomnuill —	Peak of Donald's round hollow.
Stob Coire Easain —	Peak of the round hollow of the little waterfall.
Stob Coire an t-Saighdeir —	Peak of the round hollow of the soldier.
Stob Coire an t-Sneachda —	Peak of the round hollow of the snow.
Stob a'Choire Leith —	Peak of the grey round hollow.
Stob a'Choire Mheadhoin —	Peak of the middle round hollow.
Stob a'Choire Odhair —	Peak of the dun coloured round hollow.
Stob a'Ghlas Choire —	Peak of the green round hollow.
Aonach Air Chrith —	The shaking height.
Aonach Beag —	Little height **or** ridge.
Aonach Bheinn —	Mountain ridge.
Aonach Buidhe —	Yellow height **or** ridge.
Aonach Mor —	Big height **or** ridge.

Aonach Shasuinn –	Height or ridge of England.
Arkle –	Possibly, hill of the summer residence.
Bac an Eich –	Hollow of the horse.
Am Basteir –	The baptizer.
Bidean nam Bian –	Peak of the hides or skins.
Bidean an Eoin Deirg –	Peak of the red bird.
Blath Bhalg –	Warm bag or belly.
Blaven –	Blue mountain.
Bodach Mor –	Big old man.
Bord Mor –	Big table.
Braeriach –	Brindled upper slope.
Bruach na Frithe –	Bank of the deer forest.
Buachaille Etive Beag –	Little shepherd of Etive.
Buachaille Etive Mor –	Big shepherd of Etive.
An Caisteal –	The castle.
Caisteal Abhail –	Castle death or
	castle of the apple.
Ceann Garbh –	Rough top.
An Cearcallach –	The rounded mountain.
A'Chailleach –	The old woman.
Chno Dearg –	Red mountain.
Cioch Mhor –	Big pap.
Cioch na h-Uighe –	Pap of the maiden.
Cnap a'Chleirich –	Little hill of the clergyman.
An Coileachan –	The cockerel or
	the rivulet.
Coire Dubh	Round black stormy hollow.
Fraochaidh –	
Cul Beag –	Little hill-back.
Cul nan Creagan –	Hill-back of the rocks.
Cul Mor –	Big hill-back.
Deadh Choimhead –	Good prospect.
Derry Cairngorm –	Grove or thicket of the blue cairn.
Doire Tana –	Sparse grove or thicket.
Druim na h-Achlaise –	Ridge of the armpit.
Drumderg –	Red ridge.
Druim an Fhraoich	Ridge of the soft or smooth heather.
Mhin –	
Dun Da Ghaoithe –	Hillock of the two winds.

Dun Leacainn —	Hillock with a broad slope.
Fair Bhuidhe —	Yellow height **or** hill.
Faochag —	Cranberry mountain.
Fashven —	Desolate hill.
Fiacaill Coire an t-Sneachda —	Tooth of the round hollow of the snow.
Fiacaill na Leth-Choin —	Tooth of the lurcher (kind of hunting dog).
Gairich —	Mountain of shouting **or** yelling.
Garbh Thorr —	Rough hill.
Goatfell —	Goat mountain.
Gualann —	Corner **or** shoulder of the hill.
Leabaidh an Daimh Bhuidhe —	Bed of the yellow stag.
Leac nan Cisteachan —	Flat stone of the boxes.
An Leacainn —	The broad slope.
Leacann Doire Bainnear —	Broad slope of the milky grove.
Leac Shoilleir —	Bright hillside.
Leathad an Taobhan —	Slope of the rafter **or** beam.
Leitir Finlay —	Finlay's slope.
Leum Uilleam —	William's leap.
Lurg Mhor —	Big extended ridge.
Mam Sodhail —	Round hill of barns.
Maoile Lunndaidh —	Bare hill of the boggy place.
Maol Breac —	Speckled bare hill.
Maol Buidhe —	Yellow bare hill.
Maol Chean Dearg —	Red topped bare hill.
Marsco —	Sea-gull rock.
Mona Gowan —	Mountain **or** moor of the smith.
Monameaneach —	Middle mountain **or** moor.
Monadh nam Mial —	Mountain **or** moor of the lice **or** animals.
Monadhliath —	Grey mountains **or** moors.
Moruisg —	Probably, big water mountain.
Mullach Coire a'Chuir —	Top of the round hollow of the turn **or** bend.
Mullach nan Coirean —	Top of the little round hollows.
Mullach Coire Mhic Fhearcair —	Top of Farquharson's round hollow.

Quinag –	Bucket or waterspout.
An Riabhachan –	The grey or brindled mountain.
Roinn na Beinne –	Part or division of the mountain.
An Ruadh-Stac –	The red hill.
Saval Beg –	Little barn.
Scaraben –	Mountain of the cormorant or mountain of the young sea-gull.
Schiehallion –	Traditionally, hillock of the Caledonians.
Sgairneach Mhor –	Big shrieking or howling mountain.
Sgarbh Breac –	Speckled cormorant.
Sgarbh Dubh –	Black cormorant.
Sgreadan Hill –	Shrieking hill.
Sguman Coinntich –	Mossy stack.
Sithean Mor –	Big knoll.
Sithean na Raplaich –	Hillock of the noise.
An Sleaghach –	The spear.
Sliabh an Ruigh Dhuibh –	Mountain of the black field or slope.
Slioch –	The spear.
Spidean a'Choire Leith –	Pinnacle of the grey round hollow.
Spidean Malach –	Pinnacle of the brow of the hill.
Sron a'Chaoineidh –	Lamentation point.
Sron a'Chleirich –	Point or nose of the clergyman.
Sron a'Choire Ghairbh –	Point of the rough round hollow.
An Stac –	The steep conical hill.
Stac na Cathaig –	Steep conical hill of the jackdaw.
Stac Pollaidh –	Pool hill.
Stronchullin –	Holly point.
Stuc Scardan –	Scree hill.
An Suidhe –	The seat.
Suilven –	Pillar mountain.
An Teallach –	The forge or anvil.
Tigh Mor na Seilge –	Mansion house of the hunting.
Toll Creagach –	Rocky hole or hollow.
Tom a'Bhuachaille –	Hillock of the herdsman.
Tom a'Choinnich –	Mossy hillock.
Tom Soilleir –	Clear or visible hillock.
Torr Meadhonach –	Middle hill.
Uamh Bheag –	Little cave or hollow.

A SELECTION OF STREAM AND RIVER NAMES

ALLT — A BURN or STREAM

Allt an Achaidh —	Burn of the field.
Allt nan Achaidhean —	Burn of the fields.
Allt Beitheach —	Burn of the beast.
Allt Bhlaraidh —	Burn of the rough chipped wood.
Allt a'Bhodaich —	Burn of the old man.
Allt na Cailliche —	Burn of the old woman.
Allt na Caim —	Burn of the curve.
Allt a'Chaol Ghlinne —	Burn of the narrow glen.
Allt a'Chaoruinn —	Burn of the rowan tree.
Allt Choir a'Bhalachain —	Burn of the round hollow of the young boy.
Allt a'Choire Dhuibh —	Burn of the dark round hollow.
Allt a'Chraois —	The wide open burn.
Allt Cinn Locha —	Burn of the loch head.
Allt Coire a'Bhric Mor —	Burn of the round hollow of the big trout.
Allt Coire Dubh Mor —	Burn of the big dark round hollow.
Allt Coir' an Eich —	Burn of the round hollow of the horse.
Allt Coire an Eoin —	Burn of the round hollow of the birds.
Allt Coire Mhic Fhearchair —	MacFarquhar's round hollow.
Allt Coire Odhair —	Burn of the dun-coloured round hollow.
Allt na Doire Gairbhe —	Burn of the rough thicket.
Allt an Duin —	Burn of the hillock **or** fort.
Allt an Ealaidh —	Burn of the soft stepping.
Allt na h-Eirigh —	Burn of the rising.
Allt Fionn Ghlinne —	Burn of the white **or** fair glen.
Allt a'Ghiubhais —	Burn of the fir tree.
Allt Ghlas —	The grey burn.
Allt a'Ghlas Choire —	Burn of the green round hollow.
Allt Glas Dhoire —	Burn of the green thicket.
Allt Gleann a'Chaolais —	Burn of the glen of the narrow stretch of water.
Allt Gleann na Giubhsachan —	Burn of the pine glen.

Allt Gleann nan Meann —	Burn of the kids' glen.
Allt Laire —	Burn of the mare.
Allt Lairig Eilde —	Burn of the hind's pass.
Allt na Lairige Mhoire —	Burn of the big pass.
Allt a'Mhadaidh —	Burn of the wolf.
Allt Mhuic Bheag —	Burn of the little pig.
Allt a'Mhuillin —	Burn of the mill **or** mill stream.
Allt a'Mhullaich —	Burn of the hill top.
Allt na Muic —	Burn of the pig.
Allt nan Ramh —	Burn of the wood.
Allt Riabhach —	Brindled burn.
Allt Sleibh —	Burn of the mountain.
Allt Smeoraill —	Lively burn.
Allt an t-Sneachda —	Burn of the snow.
Allt Srath a'Ghlinne —	Burn of the glen valley.
Allt an t-Strathain —	Burn of the little valley.
Allt Tarsuinn —	Cross burn.
Crom Allt —	Crooked burn.

ABHAINN or AMHAINN — A RIVER

Abhainn Beinn nan Eun —	River of the mountain of the birds.
Abhainn a'Bhealaich —	River of the mountain pass.
Abhainn Bruachaig —	River of the little bank.
Abhainn a'Chadh Bhuide —	River of the yellow narrow pass.
Amhainn a'Choire —	River of the round hollow.
Amhainn Chuaig —	River of the difficult bend.
Abhainn Dearg —	Red river.
Abhainn Dubh —	Dark **or** black river.
Abhainn an Fhasaigh —	River of the dwelling place.
Abhainn na Frithe —	River of the deer forest.
Abhainn na Fuirness —	River of the furnace.
Abhainn a'Gharbh Choire —	River of the rough round hollow.
Abhainn a'Ghiubhais Li —	River of the coloured pine.

Abhainn Gleann na Muice —	River of the pig's glen.
Abhainn an Loin —	River of the marsh **or** meadow.
Abhainn Mhor —	Big river.
Abhainn Righ —	King river.
Abhainn an t-Stratha Charnaig —	River of the rocky valley.
Abhainn an t-Srath Chuilleannaich —	River of the valley of the holly.
Abhainn Srath na Sealga —	River of the valley of the hunting.

MISCELLANEOUS STREAMS AND RIVERS

Dubh Eas —	Dark precipitous stream.
Dubh Lighe —	Dark overflowing stream.
Feochan Bheag —	Small gentle breeze.
Fionn Lighe —	White overflowing stream.
An t-Suileag —	The little eye.
Uisge nam Fichead —	Water of the twenty.
Uisge Toll a'Mhadaidh —	Water of the wolf's den.
River Ba —	River of the cow.
River Dibiedale —	Deep dale river.
River Gloy —	River of the noise **or** shouting.
River Gour —	River of the goats.
River Hurich —	River of the yew trees.
River Loy —	River of the calf.
River Sgitheach —	River of the hawthorn.

COASTAL FEATURES

The following is a small selection of names appearing in coastal features. One word frequently found on maps is RUBHA (sometimes spelt RUDHA) which means a *point* or *promontory*.

Rubha Aird Druimnich –	Point of the ridged **or** furrowed headland.
Rubha Aird an t-Sionnaich –	Fox point.
Rubha na h-Airde Uinnsinn –	Point of the headland of the ash tree.
Rubha Beag –	Small point.
Rubha a'Bhuachaille –	Herdsman's point.
Rubha nam Brathairean/ Braithrean –	Brothers point.
Rubha nan Cearc –	Hens' point.
Rubha a'Chamais –	Point of the bay.
Rubha a'Chaoil –	Point of the narrow strait.
Rubha Chaolais –	Point of the strait.
Rubha a'Choin –	Dog point.
Rubha Chuaig –	Point of the awkward curve.
Rubha nan Clach –	Point of the rocks.
Rubha Coigeach –	Coigach point. A *coigeach* is a fifth of a davach – a reference to an old system of land measure.
Rubha Creagan Dubha –	Point of the little black rock.
Rubha Dearg –	Red point.
Rubha Dubh –	Black point.
Rubha Duin Bhain –	Point of the small light coloured hill.
Rubha an Dunain –	Point of the small hill **or** fort.
Rubha na h-Easgainne –	Eel point.
Rubha na Faoilinn –	Seagull point.
Rubha na Fearn –	Point of the alder trees.
Rubha an Fhasaidh –	Protruding point.
Rubha an Fhir Leithe –	Point of the grey man.

Rubha na Gainmhich —	Point of the sandy beach.
Rubha nan Gall —	Strangers' point.
Rubha Garbh Aird —	Point of the rough headland.
Rubha an Iasgaich —	Fishing point.
Rubha nan Leacan —	Point of the steep hillsides.
Rubha Liath —	Grey point.
Rubha nam Meirleach —	Robbers' point.
Rubha na Meise Baine —	Point of the white plate.
Rubha Mor —	Big point.
Rubha Raonuill —	Ronald's point.
Rubha Reidh —	Smooth **or** level point.
Rubha an Ridire —	Knight's point.
Rubha Rodha —	Point of the water's edge.
Rubha na Roinne —	Point of the divide.
Rubha an t-Sailean —	Point of the little inlet.
Rubha nan Sgarbh —	Cormorants' point.
Rubha Thormaid —	Norman's point.
Rubha nan Tri Clach —	Point of the three stones.
Rubha na h-Uamha —	Cave point.
Aird Mhor —	Big headland.
Ardmore Point —	Point of the big headland.
Ardnave Point —	Point of the saint's headland.
Ardpatrick Point —	Point of Patrick's headland.
Camas na Ruthaig —	Bay **or** creek of the crab.
Camas Mor —	Big bay.
Sron Bheag —	Little point.
Sron Raineach —	Fern point.
Craignish Point —	Rock island point.
Duart Point —	Black point.
Cailleach Head —	Old woman's head.
Cape Wrath —	Turning point.
Leac Dhonn —	Flat brown rock.
Corrievreckan —	Whirlpool of Brecan (a legendary figure).

APPENDIX

The following is a small selection of place names and other geographical features showing the English or anglicised forms and their Gaelic equivalents.

Aberdeen —	Obair Dheathain **or** Obar Dheadhain.
Aberfeldy —	Oba(i)r Pheallaidh.
Applecross —	A'Chomraich (*The Sanctuary*).
Arbroath —	Oba(i)r Bhrothaig.
Ardgour —	Aird Ghobhar.
Argyll —	Earraghaidheal.
Barra —	Barraidh.
Benbecula —	Beinn nam Faoghla.
Caithness —	Gallaibh.
Drumnadrochit —	Druim na Drochaid.
Dundee —	Dun-Deagh.
Dunoon —	Dun-Omhain (Obhain).
Edinburgh —	Dun-Eideann.
Falkirk —	An Eaglais Bhreac.
Fort Augustus —	Cill Chuimein.
Fort William —	An Gearasdan.
Glasgow —	Glaschu.
Harris —	Na Hearadh.
Inverness —	Inbhir-Nis.
Iona —	I Chaluim Chille **or** simply *I*.
Kintail —	Ceann an t-Saile.
Kintyre —	Cinn Tire.
Kyle Akin —	Caol Acain.
Kyle of Lochalsh —	Caol Lochaillse.
Lewis —	Leodhas.
Oban —	An t-Oban.
Perth —	Peairt.
Plockton —	Am Ploc.
Portree —	Port-Righ.
Skye —	An t-Eilean Sgitheanach (Sgiathanach).
St. Andrews —	Cill-Rimhinn.
Stirling —	S(t)ruighlea.
Stornoway —	Steornabhagh.

Strontian –	Sron an t-Sithein.
Sutherland –	Cataibh.
Tarbat/Tarbert –	An Tairbeart.
Tiree –	Tir Iodh.
Tobermory –	Tobar Mhoire.
Tomintoul –	Tom an t-Sabhail.
Torridon –	Toirbheartan.
Trossachs –	Na Troiseachan.
Tyndrum –	Taigh an Droma.
Uist –	Uibhist.
Weem –	Uaimh.
The Islands –	Na h-Eileanan.
The Hebrides –	Innse Gall.
The Minch –	An Cuan Sgith.
Ben Attow –	Beinn Fhada.
Benavean –	Beinn a'Mheadhoin.
Ben Lui –	Beinn Laoigh.
Ben Nevis –	Beinn Nibheis.
Ben Wyvis –	Beinn Uais.
Mealfourvonie –	Meall Fuarmhonaidh.
Holy Loch –	An Loch Seunta.
Loch Broom –	Loch a'Bhraoin.

NOTES